P674

# Complete Poems for Children

# Books by James Reeves

*Poems for Children*
    The Wandering Moon
    Ragged Robin
    Prefabulous Animiles
    More Prefabulous Animiles

*Stories*
    The Strange Light
    Pigeons and Princesses
    Sailor Rumbelow and Britannia
    The Forbidden Forest

*Anthologies*
    The Christmas Book
    One's None
    The Merry-Go-Round
    The Rhyming River
    Orpheus
    The Poets' World
    The Modern Poets' World

*Plays*
    Mulcaster Market
    The King Who Took Sunshine

*The Bible*
    A First Bible
    The Road to a Kingdom

*For Older Readers and Adults*
    The Everlasting Circle: Folk Song Texts
    Commitment to Poetry: Essays and Broadcasts
    How to Write Poems for Children
    Teaching Poetry
    Understanding Poetry
    A Short History of English Poetry

# JAMES REEVES

## *Complete Poems for Children*

Illustrated by Edward Ardizzone

HEINEMANN · LONDON

First published Great Britain 1994
by William Heinemann Ltd
an imprint of Reed Consumer Books Limited
Michelin House, 81 Fulham Road, London SW3 6RB
and Auckland, Melbourne, Singapore and Toronto

ISBN 0 434 96917 6

A CIP catalogue record for this book is available at the British Library

Printed in Great Britain by
St Edmundsbury Press Ltd, Bury St Edmunds, Suffolk

To
Daniel James Irwin

# Contents

## The Wandering Moon (1950)

## *The Blackbird in the Lilac (1952)*

## Prefabulous Animiles (1957)

## Ragged Robin (1961)

## The Story of Jackie Thimble (1965)

## More Prefabulous Animiles (1975)

## Additional Poems

# Acknowledgements

The following poems: 'The Blackbird in the Lilac'; 'Yellow Wheels'; 'Run a Little'; 'The Two Mice'; 'If Pigs Could Fly'; 'Mick'; 'The Old Wife and the Ghost'; 'W'; 'A Pig Tale'; 'The Three Unlucky Men'; 'The Footprint'; 'The Four Letters'; 'The Ceremonial Band'; 'Explorers'; 'Bluebells and Foxgloves'; 'The Intruder'; 'The Grasshopper and the Bird'; 'Things to Remember'; 'Seeds'; 'A Garden at Night'; 'Birds in the Forest'; 'The Toadstool Wood'; 'Cows'; 'Trees in the Moonlight'; 'The Fiddler'; 'Miss Wing'; 'Mr Bellairs'; 'Mrs Golightly'; 'Little Minnie Mystery'; 'Mrs Button'; 'Mr Gilfillan'; 'My Singing Aunt'; 'Diddling'; 'Poor Rumble'; 'The Street Musician'; 'Fireworks'; 'The Statue'; 'The Piano'; 'Rum Lane'; 'Uriconium'; 'The Black Pebble'; 'Pat's Fiddle'; 'Boating'; 'Giant Thunder'; 'The Magic Seeds'; 'Pluto and Proserpine'; 'Troy'; 'The Moonlit Stream'; 'Bobadil'; 'The Three Singing Birds'; 'Kingdom Cove'; 'The Horn'; and 'Time to Go Home' are published together under the title of *The Blackbird in the Lilac* (1952) by Oxford University Press and reproduced here by kind permission of the publishers. 'Poor Jenny's Song' (1976) published in *Young Writers Tales* 7 by Macmillan Ltd, 'Gabble-Gabble' (1966) published in the *Eleanor Farjeon Book*, Hamish Hamilton, 'Kara My Tortoise' (1974) published in *Young Writers Tales 5* by Macmillan Ltd,'Domenico' (1973) was first published in *Cricket Magazine*, March 1975, Vol. 2, No. 7, by Martin Caruse Ltd, 'The Ballad of Gideon'; 'Gliders and Gulls'; 'Alexander' previously unpublished and printed here by kind permission of the Estate of James Reeves.

All the other poems were first published by William Heinemann Ltd in *The Wandering Moon* (1950), *Prefabulous Animiles* (1957), *Ragged Robin* (1961) and *More Prefabulous Animiles* (1975).

# The
# Wandering
# Moon

# The Wandering Moon

Age after age and all alone,
    She turns through endless space,
Showing the watchers on the earth
    Her round and rocky face.
Enchantment comes upon all hearts
    That feel her lonely grace.

Mount Newton is the highest peak
    Upon the wandering moon,
And there perhaps the witches dance
    To some fantastic tune,
And in the half–light cold and grey
    Their incantations croon.

And there perhaps mad creatures come
    To play at hide–and–seek
With howling apes and blundering bears
    And bats that swoop and squeak.
I cannot see what nameless things
    Go on at Newton Peak.

I cannot tell what vessels move
    Across the Nubian Sea,
Nor whether any bird alights
    On any stony tree.
A quarter of a million miles
    Divide the moon and me.

A quarter of a million miles—
   It is a fearsome way,
But ah! if we could only fly
   On some auspicious day
And land at last on Newton Peak,
   Ah then, what games we'd play!

What songs we'd sing on Newton Peak,
   On what wild journeys go
By frozen fen or burning waste,
   Or where the moon-flowers grow,
And countless strange and fearful things—
   If only we could know!

# The Snail

At sunset, when the night-dews fall,
Out of the ivy on the wall
With horns outstretched and pointed tail
Comes the grey and noiseless snail.
On ivy stems she clambers down,
Carrying her house of brown.
Safe in the dark, no greedy eye
Can her tender body spy,
While she herself, a hungry thief,
Searches out the freshest leaf.
She travels on as best she can
Like a toppling caravan.

# Spells

I dance and dance without any feet—
This is the spell of the ripening wheat.

With never a tongue I've a tale to tell—
This is the meadow-grasses' spell.

I give you health without any fee—
This is the spell of the apple-tree.

I rhyme and riddle without any book—
This is the spell of the bubbling brook.

Without any legs I run for ever—
This is the spell of the mighty river.

I fall for ever and not at all—
This is the spell of the waterfall.

Without a voice I roar aloud—
This is the spell of the thunder-cloud.

No button or seam has my white coat—
This is the spell of the leaping goat.

I can cheat strangers with never a word—
This is the spell of the cuckoo-bird.

We have tongues in plenty but speak no names—
This is the spell of the fiery flames.

The creaking door has a spell to riddle—
I play a tune without any fiddle.

# Waiting

Waiting, waiting, waiting
  For the party to begin;
Waiting, waiting, waiting
  For the laughter and din;
Waiting, waiting, waiting
  With hair just so
And clothes trim and tidy
  From top-knot to toe.
The floor is all shiny,
  The lights are ablaze;
There are sweetmeats in plenty
  And cakes beyond praise.
Oh the games and dancing,
  The tricks and the toys,
The music and the madness
  The colour and noise!
Waiting, waiting, waiting
For the first knock on the door—
Was ever such waiting,
  Such waiting before?

# Little Fan

'I don't like the look of little Fan, mother,
   I don't like her looks a little bit.
Her face—well, it's not exactly different,
   But there's something wrong with it.

'She went down to the sea-shore yesterday,
   And she talked to somebody there,
Now she won't do anything but sit
   And comb out her yellowy hair.

'Her eyes are shiny and she sings, mother,
    Like nobody ever sang before.
Perhaps they gave her something queer to eat,
    Down by the rocks on the shore.

'Speak to me, speak, little Fan dear,
    Aren't you feeling very well?
Where have you been and what are you singing,
    And what's that seaweedy smell?

'Where did you get that shiny comb, love,
    And those pretty coral beads so red?
Yesterday you had two legs, I'm certain,
    But now there's something else instead.

'I don't like the looks of little Fan, mother,
    You'd best go and close the door.
Watch now, or she'll be gone for ever
    To the rocks by the brown sandy shore.'

# *What Kind of Music?*

What kind of music does Tom like best?
    Drums and fifes and the trumpet's bray.
What kind of music does Jenny like?
    A whirling waltz-tune sweet and gay.

What music pleases Elizabeth?
    She loves a symphony solemn and grand.
What kind of music does Benny like?
    A roaring, rhythmical ragtime band.

19

But the kind of music that Mary loves
Is any little gay or comical tune,
Played on a fiddle or clarinet
That skips like a leafy stream in June.

# The Song of the Dumb Waiter

Who went to sleep in the flower-bed?
Who let the fire-dog out of the shed?

Who sailed the sauce-boat down the stream?
What did the railway-sleeper dream?

Who was it chopped the boot-tree down,
And rode the clothes-horse through the town?

# Vicary Square

In Vicary Square at Tithe-on-Trent
The houses are all different,
As if they grew by accident.
For Number One
Is full of fun

With knob and knocker
To catch the sun;
And Number Four
Looks thin and poor,
And Number Five
Looks scarce alive,
And Number Seven, though clean and neat,
Looks like a lady without any feet.
But Number Eight
Is grand and great
With two fat lions
Beside the gate,
And Number Nine
Is deuced fine,
And Number Ten
Squats like a hen.
Number Twelve
Is by itself
Like a marble clock
Upon the shelf.

Number Twenty
Has chimneys in plenty,
Twenty-Four is square and white,
And Twenty-Five leans to the right;
Twenty-Seven is long and low,
Twenty-Nine has a bow window.
Number Thirty
Is dark and dirty,
Number Forty
Is high and haughty,
Number Fifty
Is sly and shifty.
Fifty-Two
Has a door of blue,
Fifty-Three

Has a walnut-tree
And a balcony on the second floor.

After Fifty-Four
There aren't any more.

# The Grey Horse

A dappled horse stood at the edge of the meadow,
He was peaceful and quiet and grey as a shadow.
Something he seemed to be saying to me
As he stood in the shade of the chestnut tree.

'It's a wonderful morning,' he seemed to say,
'So jump on my back, and let's be away!
It's over the hedge we'll leap and fly,
And up the hill to the edge of the sky.

'For over the hill there are fields without end;
On the galloping downs we can run like the wind.
Down pathways we'll canter, by streams we'll stray,
Oh, jump on my back and let's be away!'

As I went by the meadow one fine summer morn,
The grey horse had gone like a ghost with the dawn;
He had gone like a ghost and not waited for me,
And it's over the hilltop he'd surely be.

# Roundabout

At midsummer fair on a galloping pony
We saw the last of little Tony.
He spurred her sides and said 'Hurroo!'
And over the heads of the crowd he flew.
Said the roundabout man, 'Now don't get tragic—
That boy'll come back, the horse is magic!'
Up went Tony in the blue, blue air,
Right over the top of midsummer fair,
Till the roundabout music he heard no more,
And he set his course for the southern shore.
He saw the houses, row on row,
And he heard the cocks in the farms below.

Trees and rivers went sliding by
As the pony sailed through the blue, blue sky.
He saw the ships and the coast of France
And sailor-boys in a hornpipe dance.
He passed strange birds which he shouted to,
And away to the south he flew and flew.
Night came on and another day
And still he flew to the south away.
On and on at a galloping speed
Went little Tony and his roundabout steed.
Churches he saw and castles and towns,
Mountains and forests, dales and downs.
They crossed the Mediterranean Sea
And they came to the coast of Afrikee.
And there were palm-trees and black men bare,
All hot and hazy in the tropical air,
And lone grey mountains and deserts brown
And giant cataracts tumbling down,
Giraffes and lions and chimpanzees
And monkeys swinging among the trees.
He never felt hungry, did little Tony,
Sitting astride his magic pony,
But after a while the marvellous beast
Changed its course and made for the east,
And they came to an island in the sea
Not far from the shores of Afrikee.
So they lighted down and soon they stood
On a wild hillside by a little wood.
After a while a tall man came
Who gave them food and told them his name.
And there they'll stay for a year or more
Where never a white boy stayed before.
There in the sun lives little Tony
With the friendly people and the magic pony.
One of these days he will say good-bye
And rise aloft in the blue, blue sky,

And gallop away through the air once more
Till he lands at last on his native shore.
So you see what marvellous things and rare
Can chance to a boy at midsummer fair.

# Grim and Gloomy

Oh, grim and gloomy,
So grim and gloomy
Are the caves beneath the sea.
Oh, rare but roomy
And bare and boomy,
Those salt sea caverns be.

Oh, slim and slimy
Or grey and grimy
Are the animals of the sea.
Salt and oozy
And safe and snoozy
The caves where those animals be.

Hark to the shuffling,
Huge and snuffling,
Ravenous, cavernous, great sea-beasts!
But fair and fabulous,
Tintinnabulous,
Gay and fabulous are their feasts.

Ah, but the queen of the sea,
The querulous, perilous sea!
How the curls of her tresses
The pearls on her dresses,

Sway and swirl in the waves,
How cosy and dozy,
How sweet ring-a-rosy
Her bower in the deep-sea caves!

Oh, rare but roomy
And bare and boomy
Those caverns under the sea,
And grave and grandiose,
Safe and sandiose
The dens of her denizens be.

# Old Moll

The moon is up,
  The night owls scritch.
Who's that croaking?
  The frog in the ditch.
Who's that howling?
  The old hound bitch.
My neck tingles,
  My elbows itch,
My hair rises,
  My eyelids twitch.
What's in that pot
  So rare and rich?
Who's that crouching
  In a cloak like pitch?
Hush! that's Old Moll—
  They say she's a
Most ree-markable old party.

# The Four Horses

White Rose is a quiet horse
   For a lady to ride,
Jog-trotting on the high road
   Or through the countryside.

Grey Wolf is a hunter
   All muscle and fire;
Day long he will gallop
   And not tumble or tire.

Black Magic's a race-horse;
   She is gone like a ghost,
With the wind in her mane
   To whirl past the post.

But munching his fill
   In a field of green clover
Stands Brownie the cart-horse,
   Whose labour is over.

# Tree Gowns

In the morning her dress is of palest green,
And in dark green in the heat of noon is she seen.
At evening she puts on a dress of rich gold,
But at night this poor lady is bare and cold.

# Grey

Grey is the sky, and grey the woodman's cot
With grey smoke tumbling from the chimney-pot.
The flagstones are grey that lead to the door;
Grey is the hearth, and grey the worn old floor.

The old man by the fire nods in his chair;
Grey are his clothes and silvery grey his hair.
Grey are the shadows around him creeping,
And grey the mouse from the corner peeping.

# Mr Tom Narrow

A scandalous man
    Was Mr Tom Narrow,
He pushed his grandmother
    Round in a barrow.
And he called out loud
    As he rang his bell,
'Grannies to sell!
    Old grannies to sell!'

The neighbours said,
   As they heard his cry
'This poor old lady
   We will not buy.
He surely must be
   A mischievous man
To try for to sell
   His own dear Gran.'

'Besides,' said another,
   'If you ask me,
She'd be very small use
   That I can see.'
'You're right,' said a third,
   'And no mistake—
A very poor bargain
   She'd surely make.'

So Mr Tom Narrow
   He scratched his head,
And he sent his grandmother
   Back to bed;
And he rang his bell
   Through all the town
Till he sold his barrow
   For half a crown.

# Animals' Houses

Of animals' houses
    Two sorts are found—
Those which are square ones
    And those which are round.

Square is a hen-house,
    A kennel, a sty:
Cows have square houses
    And so have I.

A snail's shell is curly,
    A bird's nest round;
Rabbits have twisty burrows
    Underground.

But the fish in the bowl
    And the fish at sea—
Their houses are round
    As a house can be.

# Fire

Hard and black is my home,
Hard as a rock and black as night.
Scarlet and gold am I,
Delicate, warm and bright.

For long years I lie,
A prisoner in the dark,
Till at last I break my fetters
In a rush of flame and spark.

First a tree and then a rock
The house where I sleep.
Now like a demon
I crackle and hiss and leap.

# Caroline, Caroline

Caroline, Caroline sing me a song.
Let it be a little one or let it be long.
Whether you make me weep, or make me rejoice,
Here's a silver shilling to raise up your voice.

Sing me what the mermaids sing in their sandy caves
Or sing me the birds' song from over the waves.
Sing me a sailors' song from far, far away,
Or your own little song of derry-down-day.

Play me the music of the rain on the hill,
Or play any music, any music you will.
Caroline, Caroline sing to me and play,
And I will join in with your derry-down-day.

# A Mermaid Song

She sits by the sea in the clear, shining air,
    And the sailors call her Moonlight, Moonlight;
They see her smoothing her wavy hair
    And they hear her singing, singing.
The sea-shells learn their tunes from her
And the big fish listen with never a stir
    To catch the voice of Moonlight, Moonlight,
And I would hark for a year and a year
    To hear her singing, singing.

# A Farthing and a Penny

For a farthing and a penny you cannot buy much,
You cannot buy a parrot nor rabbits in a hutch.
You can buy sugary sweets but not very many,
Oh what shall I buy with my farthing and a penny?

# Mrs Farleigh-Fashion

Mrs Farleigh-Fashion
Flies into a passion
If any frock is finer than hers.
How she bobs and bounces
In her fleecy flounces,
She is like a queen in her feathers and furs.

She has a gown of flame,
Which puts ours to shame,
And one that billows like the boisterous sea.
She has another of silk,
White as morning milk,
That sighs and whispers like wind in a tree.

Mrs Farleigh-Fashion
With a long lilac sash on
Waltzed with the General at the County Ball.
When that great man of war
Fell senseless to the floor
We had to own she had conquered us all.

# The Wind

I can get through a doorway without any key,
And strip the leaves from the great oak tree.

I can drive storm-clouds and shake tall towers,
Or steal through a garden and not wake the flowers.

Seas I can move and ships I can sink;
I can carry a house-top or the scent of a pink.

When I am angry I can rave and riot;
And when I am spent, I lie quiet as quiet.

# Under Ground

In the deep kingdom under ground
There is no light and little sound.

Down below the earth's green floor
The rabbit and the mole explore.

The quarrying ants run to and fro
To make their populous empires grow.

Do they, as I pass overhead,
Stop in their work to hear my tread?

Some creatures sleep and do not toil,
Secure and warm beneath the soil.

Sometimes a fork or spade intrudes
Upon their earthy solitudes.

Downward the branching tree-roots spread
Into the country of the dead.

Deep down, the buried rocks and stones
Are like the earth's gigantic bones.

In the dark kingdom under ground
How many marvellous things are found!

# Slowly

Slowly the tide creeps up the sand,
Slowly the shadows cross the land.
Slowly the cart-horse pulls his mile,
Slowly the old man mounts the stile.

Slowly the hands move round the clock,
Slowly the dew dries on the dock.
Slow is the snail—but slowest of all
The green moss spreads on the old brick wall.

# The Summer Party

In a blue, blue bonnet
With posies on it
Came Mrs Muckle
To the summer party.
With tight, bright boots on
And festive suits on
Came Mr Hearty
And old Dr Hearty.

The divinest creatures
With their rare, soft features
Were Lady Charlotte
And her sister Bramble.
Not quite so pretty
But a deal more witty
Were the sprightly nieces
Of Captain Campbell.

Oh brave, brave the dresses
Triumphant the tresses
Of Rose Arabella,
Susannah and Sally.
Of renown and talent,
As handsome as gallant,
Were the cavaliers
Who attended the rally.

Sweet, sweet was the weather
For walking together
In twos on the lawn,
A dame and a dandy.
And Lady Dinah
Took tea from old china,
Sandwiches too,
And cream cakes and candy.

Gay, gay was the clinking
Of cups and the drinking
Of cordial glasses
Of lemon and lime.
Oh merry the fluting,
The scraping and tooting,
The lovely music
They made at that time.

See, see how entrancing
And careless the dancing,
Oh, what temptation
Through rose-beds to ramble!
Mrs Muckle's daughter
Has gone on the water
In a little boat
With brave Captain Campbell.

Long, long will the faces,
The grandeur and graces
Of those dear ladies
Be remembered hereafter.
Even Mrs Vapour
To see such a caper
Could scarcely resist
To join in the laughter.

Some half-dozen heroes,
Bold, bold cavalieros
Went on to a tavern
For a glass or two more;
And there it was voted
That never more noted
Summer assembly
Had been gathered before.

# Doctor Emmanuel

Doctor Emmanuel Harrison-Hyde
Has a very big head with brains inside.
I wonder what happens inside the brains
That Doctor Emmanuel's head contains.

# Miss Petal

Sweet Miss Petal,
She sings like a kettle,
  Tra-la!
Dancing, dancing
Wherever she goes,
She twirls about
On the points of her toes.
  Tra-la!
Like a moth she dances
On fluttery wings,
Like a silver kettle
She bubbles and sings,
  Tra-la!
Neat she is
Like a little white rose,
Twirling about
On the points of her toes,
Flitting and trilling
Wherever she goes,
  Tra-la!
Dear Miss Petal,
If only she'd settle—
  But no!
From morn till night,
Day in day out,
She turns and turns
Like a roundabout.
If only, if only
She'd come to rest

Like a bee on a bush,
A bird on a nest.
If only, if only
She'd sit and settle,
Like a sensible, sober,
Sweet Miss Petal—
  But no!
Away she goes
On her twinkling toes,
High on her toes
Like a tippling top,
And nobody knows
If sweet Miss Petal
Who sings like a kettle
Will ever settle
  And stop!

# Mr Kartoffel

Mr Kartoffel's a whimsical man;
He drinks his beer from a watering-can,
And for no good reason that I can see
He fills his pockets with china tea.
He parts his hair with a knife and fork
And takes his ducks for a Sunday walk.
Says he, 'If my wife and I should choose
To wear our stockings outside our shoes,
Plant tulip-bulbs in the baby's pram
And eat tobacco instead of jam,
And fill the bath with cauliflowers,
That's nobody's business at all but ours.'

Says Mrs K., 'I may choose to travel
With a sack of grass or a sack of gravel,
Or paint my toes, one black, one white,
Or sit on a birds' nest half the night—
But whatever I do that is rum or rare,
I rather think that it's my affair.
So fill up your pockets with stamps and string,
And let us be ready for anything!'
Says Mr K. to his whimsical wife,
'How can we face the storms of life,
Unless we are ready for anything?
So if you've provided the stamps and string,
Let us pump up the saddle and harness the horse
And fill him with carrots and custard and sauce,
Let us leap on him lightly and give him a shove
And it's over the sea and away, my love!'


# Rabbit and Lark

'Under the ground
    It's rumbly and dark
And interesting,'
    Said Rabbit to Lark.

Said Lark to Rabbit,
    'Up in the sky
There's plenty of room
    And it's airy and high.'

'Under the ground
    It's warm and dry.
Won't you live with me?'
    Was Rabbit's reply.

'The air's so sunny.
   I wish you'd agree,'
Said the little Lark,
   'To live with me.'

But under the ground
   And up in the sky,
Larks can't burrow
   Nor rabbits fly.

So Skylark over
   And Rabbit under
They had to settle
   To live asunder.

And often these two friends
   Meet with a will
For a chat together
   On top of the hill.


# The Musical Box

Mary, Mary come and listen a minute!
Here's a little wooden box with music in it.
There are little bells inside, and they tinkle and play,
And 'Early One Morning' are the words they say.

Early one morning to the woods we will run,
And see the sweet flowers at the rising of the sun.
We will join hands together and dance in a ring
And 'The Bluebells of Scotland' is the tune we will sing.

The bluebells of Scotland they jingle merrily,
And the tune that they ring is 'The Miller of Dee'.
The jolly, jolly miller, he whistles as he goes,
And 'The Merry Widow Waltz' is the best tune he
    knows.

The merry, merry widow, she loves to sing and play,
And the song that she sings is 'The Vicar of Bray'.
Oh, hear the vicar sing with his mellow mellow voice,
And 'Bonnie Annie Laurie' is the song of his choice.

Annie, she can sing and dance like a fairy,
And the song she loves best of all is 'Mary, Mary'.
Mary, Mary, come and listen a minute!
Here's a little wooden box with music in it.

# Dr John Hearty

Dr John Hearty,
　　Though old as a fossil,
Could dance like a fairy
　　And sing like a throstle.

He had not a tooth left
　　To ache and decay,
And his hair, white as snow,
　　Had melted away.

He had lived in this world
　　A weary long while,
And all that he saw in it
　　Caused him to smile.

For shocking they might be,
　　The things that he saw,
But old Dr Hearty
　　Had seen worse before.

He had patients in plenty
　　So deathly and grim,
But their ills were all cured
　　With laughing at him.

For Dr John Hearty
　　Though old as a fossil,
Would dance like a fairy
　　And sing like a throstle.

# *Musetta of the Mountains*

Musetta of the mountains
  She lives amongst the snow,
Coming and going softly
  On a white doe.
Her face is pale and smiling
  Her hair is of gold;
She wears a red mantle
  To keep her from the cold.

Musetta of the mountains,
  She rides in the night
On her swift-footed doe
  So gentle and light;
In the frosty starlight
  Sometimes you may hear
The bells on its bridle
  Far away but clear.

Sometimes from the far snows
  The winter wind brings
The thin voice of Musetta,
  And this is what she sings:
'Follow me and follow me
  And come to my mountains.
I will show you eagles' nests
  By the frozen fountains.

'Death-cold are the high peaks
  Of the mountains lone,
But a marvellous sight
  Is the snow-queen's throne.
Death-cold are the mountains
  And the winds sharp as spite,
But warm is the welcome
  In my cabin at night.'

Thus sings Musetta
  In the frosty air,
While the delicate snowflakes
  Light on her hair.
But there is none to follow her,
  No one to ride
Away with fair Musetta
  To the far mountain-side.

## Queer Things

'Very, very queer things have been happening to me
  In some of the places where I've been.
I went to the pillar-box this morning with a letter
  And a hand came out and took it in.

'When I got home again, I thought I'd have
  A glass of spirits to steady myself;
And I take my bible oath, but that bottle and glass
  Came a-hopping down off the shelf.

'No, no, I says, I'd better take no spirits,
    And I sat down to have a cup of tea;
And blowed if my old pair of carpet-slippers
    Didn't walk across the carpet to me!

'So I took my newspaper and went into the park,
    And looked 'round to see no one was near,
When a voice right out of the middle of the paper
    Started reading the news bold and clear!

'Well, I guess there's some magician out to help me,
    So perhaps there's no need for alarm;
And if I manage not to anger him,
    Why should he do me any harm?'

# Stocking and Shirt

Stocking and shirt
  Can trip and prance,
Though nobody's in them
  To make them dance.
See how they waltz
  Or minuet,
Watch the petticoat
  Pirouette.
This is the dance
  Of stocking and shirt,
When the wind puts on
  The white lace skirt.
Old clothes and young clothes
  Dance together,
Twirling and whirling
  In the mad March weather.
'Come!' cries the wind,
  To stocking and shirt.
'Away!' cries the wind
  To blouse and skirt.
Then clothes and wind
  All pull together,
Tugging like mad
  In the mad March weather.
Across the garden
  They suddenly fly
And over the far hedge
  High, high, high!

'Stop!' cries the housewife,
But all too late,
Her clothes have passed
The furthest gate.
They are gone for ever
In the bright blue sky,
And only the handkerchiefs
Wave good-bye.

# Mrs Utter

Poor Mrs Utter,
She eats no butter,
But gristly meat and horrible pies,
With a mug of sour ale
And a loaf that is stale
And a withered brown fish with buttony eyes!

In a black tattered skirt
She kneels in the dirt
And clatters her dustpan and brush on the stairs;
But everything's dusty
And musty and rusty,
For the pump-handle's broken, the broom has no hairs.

The roof-top is leaky,
The window-frames squeaky,
And out of the chimney the fledgelings fly.
Beside the bare grate
Lies old scraggy Kate,
A cat with one ear and one emerald eye.

Poor Mrs Utter
    Would mumble and mutter,
'Ah! this is no life for a Princess of Spain.
    I once had fine fare
    And silk clothes to wear.
Ah me, shall I ever be rich again?'


# *Bells*

Hard as crystal,
    Clear as an icicle,
Is the tinkling sound
    Of a bell on a bicycle.

The bell in the clock
   That stands on the shelf
Slowly, sleepily
   Talks to itself.

The school bell is noisy
   And bangs like brass.
'Hurry up! Hurry up!
   Late for class!'

But deep and distant
   And peaceful to me
Are the bells I hear
   Below the sea.

Lying by the sea-shore
   On a calm day
Sometimes I hear them
   Far, far away.

With solemn tune
   In stately time
Under the water
   I hear them chime.

Why do the bells
   So stately sound?
For a sea-king dead,
   A sailor drowned?

Hark, how they peal
   Far, far away!
Is it a mermaid's
   Marriage-day?

Do they ring for joy
　　Or weeping or war,
Those bells I hear
　　As I lie by the shore?

But merry or mournful
　　So sweet to me
Are those dreamy bells
　　Below the sea.

# *Shiny*

Shiny are the chestnut leaves
　　Before they unfold.
The inside of a buttercup
　　Is like polished gold.
A pool in the sunshine
　　Is bright too,
And a fine silver shilling
　　When it is new.
But the round, full moon,
　　So clear and white,
How brightly she shines
　　On a winter night!
Slowly she rises,
　　Higher and higher,
With a cold clear light
　　Like ice on fire.

# The Grasses

The grasses nod together
   In the field where I play,
And I can never quite catch
   What they whisper and say.
Sometimes their talk
   Seems friendly and wise,
Sometimes they speak of me
   With gossip and lies.

# Stones by the Sea

Smooth and flat, grey, brown and white,
Winter and summer, noon and night,
Tumbling together for a thousand ages,
We ought to be wiser than Eastern sages.
But no doubt we stones are foolish as most,
So we don't say much on our stretch of coast.
Quiet and peaceful we mainly sit,
And when storms come up we grumble a bit.

# You'd Say it was a Wedding

You'd say it was a wedding,
   So glib and gay the talk is,
When old Mr Dorkis
   Goes out with Mrs Dorkis.

Of horses, carts, carriages,
Birthdays and marriages,
Of old friends and foes,
Of windfalls and woes,
Of bad luck and good luck
With cow, calf, chicken or duck—
Of such is their talk
When they go for a walk.

As many are the jokes
Of old Mr Dorkis
As a wheel has spokes
Or a pig porkers.

# You'd Say it was a Funeral

You'd say it was a funeral, a funeral,
    So dreary and so dim,
    So ghoulish and so grim
Is the conversation, the conversation
    Of Mr and Mrs Mimm.

Of accidents, bad accidents,
    Of widows, wars and wills,
Of tragedy, dark tragedy,
    And chills and pills and bills,
    Of doctoring and lawyering
    And quarrelling so dire,
Of burying, sad burying,
    And farms on fire.
Of sickness and starvation
    And all things grave and grim,
Of such is the conversation
    Of Mr and Mrs Mimm.

# Beech Leaves

In autumn down the beechwood path
  The leaves lie thick upon the ground.
It's there I love to kick my way
  And hear their crisp and crashing sound.

I am a giant, and my steps
  Echo and thunder to the sky.
How the small creatures of the woods
  Must quake and cower as I pass by!

This brave and merry noise I make
  In summer also when I stride
Down to the shining, pebbly sea
  And kick the frothing waves aside.

# The Two Old Women of Mumbling Hill

*The two old trees on Mumbling Hill,*
*They whisper and chatter and never keep still.*
*What do they say as they lean together*
*In rain or sunshine or windy weather?*

There were two old women lived near the hill,
And they used to gossip as women will
Of friends and neighbours, houses and shops,
Weather and trouble and clothes and crops.

And one sad winter they both took ill,
The two old women of Mumbling Hill.
They were bent and feeble and wasted away
And both of them died on the selfsame day.

Now the ghosts of the women of Mumbling Hill,
They started to call out loud and shrill,
'Where are the tales we used to tell,
And where is the talking we loved so well?'

Side by side stood the ghosts until
They both took root on Mumbling Hill;
And they turned to trees, and they slowly grew,
Summer and winter the long years through.

In the winter the bare boughs creaked and cried,
In summer the green leaves whispered and sighed;
And still they talk of fine and rain,
Storm and sunshine, comfort and pain.

The two old trees of Mumbling Hill,
They whisper and chatter and never keep still.
What do they say as they lean together
In rain or sunshine or windy weather?

# Others

'Mother, oh mother! where shall we hide us?
Others there are in the house beside us—
Moths and mice and crooked brown spiders!'

## Snow Palace

Beside a black and frozen lake
    The palace of the Queen of Snow
Is guarded by the pointed peaks
    Of icy mountains row on row.
And in the moonlight cold and keen
    Like giants huge the mountains stand
Each with his spear of deadly steel
    Gripped hard within his loyal hand.


## Village Sounds

Lie on this green and close your eyes—
    A busy world you'll hear
Of noises high and low, and loud
    And soft, and far and near.

Amidst the squawking geese and ducks,
    And hens that cluck and croon,
The rooster on the dung-hill sings
    His shrill, triumphant tune.

A watch-dog barks to scare away
　　Some sudden passer-by;
The dog wakes Mrs Goodman's Jane
　　And she begins to cry.

And now the crying babe is still,
　　You hear young blacksmith George
Din-dinning on his anvil bright
　　Far off in his black forge.

Then on his tinkling cycle comes
　　The postman with his load,
And motor-buses sound their horns
　　Upon the London Road.

Sometimes a hay-cart rumbles past,
　　The old sow grunts and stirs,
And in John Farrow's timber-yard
　　The engine throbs and whirrs.

Just across there the schoolroom stands,
　　And from the open door
You hear the sound of 'Billy Boy'
　　Or else of four times four.

At half-past-three a sudden noise—
　　The children come from school,
And shouting to the meadow run
　　To play beside the pool.

And then, when all these sounds are still
　　In the hot afternoon,
As you lie on the quiet green
　　You'll hear my favourite tune.

Down from the green boughs overhead
    The gentlest murmurs float,
As hour by hour the pigeon coos
    His soft contented note.

# The Castle

One day I built a castle in the sand,
    With battlements and pointed turret crowned.
The tide came up, my mother called me home,
    And so I left my castle to be drowned.

That night I dreamed how in my castle tower
    There stood a maid, distracted and forlorn,
Who wrung her white hands, praying for the sound
    Of horse's hooves and the deliverer's horn.

# The Sea

The sea is a hungry dog,
Giant and grey.
He rolls on the beach all day.
With his clashing teeth and shaggy jaws
Hour upon hour he gnaws

The rumbling, tumbling stones,
And 'Bones, bones, bones, bones!'
The giant sea-dog moans,
Licking his greasy paws.

And when the night wind roars
And the moon rocks in the stormy cloud,
He bounds to his feet and snuffs and sniffs,
Shaking his wet sides over the cliffs,
And howls and hollos long and loud.

But on quiet days in May or June,
When even the grasses on the dune
Play no more their reedy tune,
With his head between his paws
He lies on the sandy shores,
So quiet, so quiet, he scarcely snores.

# The Blackbird in the Lilac

# The Blackbird

## in the Lilac

# The Blackbird in the Lilac

'Good fortune!' and 'Good fortune!'
I heard the blackbird in the lilac say,
As I set out upon the road to somewhere,
  That sunny summer's day.

Gay ribbons and sad ballads
And suchlike things I carried in my pack,
But thought of home was heavier than the load
  I had upon my back.

'Come buy, come buy, fine people!'
I cried on bridges and in market squares;
On village greens I showed my toys and trifles,
  But none would have my wares.

Yet still I sing my ballads,
And think of home, and go where fortune leads.
Homewards I will not turn without good fortune,
  Though none my singing heeds.

For still I hear the blackbird
Wish me good fortune from the lilac sweet:
Such songs as his, amid the summer's promise,
  Could never be deceit.

# Dance

# and Rhyme

# Yellow Wheels

A yellow gig has Farmer Patch;
  He drives a handsome mare—
Two bright wheels and four bright hooves
  To carry him to the fair.

Yellow wheels, where are you off to,
  Twinkling down the lane,
Sparkling in the April sunshine
  And the April rain?

Farmer Patch we do not love;
  He wears a crusty frown.
But how we love to see his gig
  Go spanking off to town!

Yellow wheels, where are you off to,
  Twinkling down the lane,
Sparkling in the April sunshine
  And the April rain?

# Run a Little

===

Run a little this way,
    Run a little that!
Fine new feathers
    For a fine new hat.
A fine new hat
    For a lady fair—
Run round and turn about
    And jump in the air.

Run a little this way,
    Run a little that!
White silk ribbon
    For a black silk cat.
A black silk cat
    For the Lord Mayor's wife—
Run around and turn about
    And fly for your life!

# The Two Mice

===

There met two mice at Scarborough
    Beside the rushing sea,
The one from Market Harborough,
    The other from Dundee.

They shook their feet, they clapped their hands,
　　And twirled their tails about;
They danced all day upon the sands
　　Until the stars peeped out.

'I'm much fatigued,' the one mouse sighed,
　　'And ready for my tea.'
'Come hame awa',' the other cried,
　　'And tak' a crumb wi' me.'

They slept awhile, and then next day
　　Across the moors they went;
But sad to say, they lost their way
　　And came to Stoke-on-Trent.

And there it soon began to rain,
　　At which they cried full sore:
'If ever we get home again,
　　We'll not go dancing more.'

# If Pigs Could Fly

If pigs could fly, I'd fly a pig
To foreign countries small and big—
　　To Italy and Spain,
To Austria, where cowbells ring,
To Germany, where people sing—
　　And then come home again.

I'd see the Ganges and the Nile;
I'd visit Madagascar's isle,
　　And Persia and Peru.

People would say they'd never seen
So odd, so strange an air-machine
   As that on which I flew.

Why, everyone would raise a shout
To see his trotters and his snout
   Come floating from the sky;
And I would be a famous star
Well known in countries near and far—
   If only pigs could fly!


## Mick

Mick my mongrel-O
   Lives in a bungalow,
Painted green with a round doorway.
   With an eye for cats
   And a nose for rats
He lies on his threshold half the day.
   He buries his bones
   By the rockery stones,
And never, oh never, forgets the place,
   Ragged and thin
   From his tail to his chin,
He looks at you with a sideways face.
   Dusty and brownish,
   Wicked and clownish,
He'll win no prize at the County Show.
   But throw him a stick,
   And up jumps Mick,
And right through the flower-beds see him go!

# The Old Wife and the Ghost

There was an old wife and she lived all alone
    In a cottage not far from Hitchin:
And one bright night, by the full moon light,
    Comes a ghost right into her kitchen.

About that kitchen neat and clean
    The ghost goes pottering round.
But the poor old wife is deaf as a boot
    And so hears never a sound.

The ghost blows up the kitchen fire,
    As bold as bold can be;
He helps himself from the larder shelf,
    But never a sound hears she.

He blows on his hands to make them warm,
    And whistles aloud 'Whee-hee!'
But still as a sack the old soul lies
    And never a sound hears she.

From corner to corner he runs about,
    And into the cupboard he peeps;
He rattles the door and bumps on the floor,
    But still the old wife sleeps.

Jangle and bang go the pots and pans,
    As he throws them all around;
And the plates and mugs and dishes and jugs,
    He flings them all to the ground.

Madly the ghost tears up and down
    And screams like a storm at sea;
And at last the old wife stirs in her bed—
    And it's 'Drat those mice,' says she.

Then the first cock crows and morning shows
    And the troublesome ghost's away.
But oh! what a pickle the poor wife sees
    When she gets up next day.

'Them's tidy big mice,' the old wife thinks,
    And off she goes to Hitchin,
And a tidy big cat she fetches back
    To keep the mice from her kitchen.

# W

The King sent for his wise men all
    To find a rhyme for W;
When they had thought a good long time
But could not think of a single rhyme,
    'I'm sorry,' said he, 'to trouble you.'

# A Pig Tale

Poor Jane Higgins,
    She had five piggins,
And one got drowned in the Irish Sea.
    Poor Jane Higgins,
    She had four piggins,
And one flew over a sycamore tree.
    Poor Jane Higgins,
    She had three piggins,
And one was taken away for pork.
    Poor Jane Higgins,
    She had two piggins,
And one was sent to the Bishop of Cork.
    Poor Jane Higgins,
    She had one piggin,
And that was struck by a shower of hail,
    So poor Jane Higgins,
    She had no piggins,
And that's the end of my little pig tale.

# The Three Unlucky Men

Near Wookey Hole in days gone by
    Lived three unlucky men.
The first fell down a Treacle Mine
    And never stirred again.

The second had no better fate
    And he too is no more.
He fell into a Custard Lake
    And could not get to shore.

The third poor fellow, sad to say,
    He had no fairer luck,
For he climbed up a Porridge Hill
    And half-way down got stuck.

Alas, alas! man is but grass,
    Let life be short or long;
And all the birds cried 'Fancy that!'
    To hear this merry song.

# The Footprint

Poor Crusoe saw with fear-struck eyes
    The footprint on the shore—
Oh! what is this that shines so clear
    Upon the bathroom floor?

# The Four Letters

N,
  S,
    W,
      and E—
These are the letters which I can see
High on top of the old grey church
Where the golden rooster has his perch.
What they mean I do not know,
Though somebody told me long ago.
It might be that and it might be this,
But here is what I *think* it is:
N for Nowhere, S for Somewhere,
E for everywhere, and W for Where—
And if I am wrong, I don't much care.

# The Ceremonial Band

(*To be said out loud by a chorus and solo voices*)

The old King of Dorchester,
He had a little orchestra,
And never did you hear such a ceremonial band.
   'Tootle-too,' said the flute,
   'Deed-a-reedle,' said the fiddle,
For the fiddles and the flutes were the finest in the land.

The old King of Dorchester,
He had a little orchestra,
And never did you hear such a ceremonial band.
   'Pump-a-rum,' said the drum,
   'Tootle-too,' said the flute,
   'Deed-a-reedle,' said the fiddle,
For the fiddles and the flutes were the finest in the land.

The old King of Dorchester,
He had a little orchestra,
And never did you hear such a ceremonial band.
   'Pickle-pee,' said the fife,
   'Pump-a-rum,' said the drum,
   'Tootle-too,' said the flute,
   'Deed-a-reedle,' said the fiddle,
For the fiddles and the flutes were the finest in the land.

The old King of Dorchester,
He had a little orchestra,
And never did you hear such a ceremonial band.
   'Zoomba-zoom,' said the bass,
   'Pickle-pee,' said the fife,

'Pump-a-rum,' said the drum,
'Tootle-too,' said the flute,
'Deed-a-reedle,' said the fiddle,
For the fiddles and the flutes were the finest in the land.

The old King of Dorchester,
He had a little orchestra,
And never did you hear such a ceremonial band.
'Pah-pa-rah,' said the trumpet,
'Zoomba-zoom,' said the bass,
'Pickle-pee,' said the fife,
'Pump-a-rum,' said the drum,
'Tootle-too,' said the flute,
'Deed-a-reedle,' said the fiddle,
For the fiddles and the flutes were the finest in the land,
Oh! the fiddles and the flutes were the finest in the land!

# Hedge

## and Harvest

# Explorers

The furry moth explores the night,
  The fish discover cities drowned,
And moles and worms and ants explore
  The many cupboards underground.

The soaring lark explores the sky,
  And gulls explore the stormy seas.
The busy squirrel rummages
  Among the attics of the trees.

# Bluebells and Foxgloves

If bluebells could be rung
  In early summer time,
The sound you'd hear would be
  A small, silvery chime.

The bells on foxglove spires,
  If they could once be tolled,
Would give a mellow sound
  As deep and rich as gold.

The bluebells and foxgloves—
　If they together pealed,
Who knows what elfin footsteps
　Would crowd across the field?


# The Intruder

Two-boots in the forest walks,
Pushing through the bracken stalks.

Vanishing like a puff of smoke,
Nimbletail flies up the oak.

Longears helter-skelter shoots
Into his house among the roots.

At work upon the highest bark,
Tapperbill knocks off to hark.

Painted-wings through sun and shade
Flounces off along the glade.

Not a creature lingers by,
When clumping Two-boots comes to pry.

# The Grasshopper and the Bird

The grasshopper said
To the bird in the tree
  Zik-a-zik zik-a-zik
As polite as could be—
  Zik-a-zik zik-a-zik—
Which he meant for to say
In his grasshopper way
For the time of the year
'Twas a *vairy* warm day—
  Zik-a-zik zik-a-zik—
What a very warm day!

  Tee-oo-ee tee-oo-ee
Said the bird in the tree,
  Tee-oo-ee tee-oo-ee
As polite as could be;
That's as much as to say—
  Tee-oo-ee tee-oo-ee
That I can't quite agree!
So he upped with his wings—
  Tee-oo-ee tee-oo-ee
And he flew from the tree.

So the grasshopper hopped
Four hops and away
  Snick!
    Click!
      Flick!
        Slick!—
Four hops and away
To the edge of the hay
  Zik-a-zik zik-a-zik
For the rest of the day.

  Zik-a-zik zik-a-zik
  Tee-oo-ee tee-oo-ee
The bird and the grasshopper
Can't quite agree.

# *Things to Remember*

The buttercups in May,
The wild rose on the spray,
The poppy in the hay,

The primrose in the dell,
The freckled foxglove bell,
The honeysuckle's smell

Are things I would remember
When cheerless, raw November
Makes room for dark December.

# Seeds

A row of pearls
Delicate green
Cased in white velvet—
The broad bean.

Smallest of birds
Winged and brown,
Seed of the maple
Flutters down.

Cupped like an egg
Without a yolk,
Grows the acorn,
Seed of the oak.

Autumn the housewife
Now unlocks
Seeds of the poppy
In their spice-box.

Silver hair
From an old man's crown
Wind-stolen
Is thistledown.

# A Garden at Night

On powdery wings the white moths pass,
And petals fall on the dewy grass;
Over the bed where the poppy sleeps
The furtive fragrance of lavender creeps.
Here lived an old lady in days long gone,
And the ghost of that lady lingers on.
She sniffs the roses, and seems to see
The ripening fruit on the orchard tree;
Like the scent of flowers her spirit weaves
Its winding way through the maze of leaves;
Up and down like the moths it goes:
Never and never it finds repose.
Gentle she was, and quiet and kind,
But flitting and restless was her old mind.
So hither and thither across the lawn
Her spirit wanders, till grey of dawn
Rouses the cock in the valley far,
And the garden waits for the morning star.

# Birds in the Forest

Birds in the forest sing
   Of meadows green;
They sing of primrose banks
   With pools between.

Birds of the forest sing
   Of gardens bright;
They sing of scented flowers
   That haunt the night.

Birds in the forest sing
   Of falling water,
Falling like the hair
   Of a king's daughter.

Birds in the forest sing
   Of foreign lands;
They sing of hills beyond
   The foamy sands.

They sing of a far mountain
   Topped by a town
Where sits a grey wizard
   In a gold crown.

The songs the wild birds sing
   In forests tall,
It was the old grey wizard
   Taught them all.

# The Toadstool Wood

The toadstool wood is dark and mouldy,
    And has a ferny smell.
About the trees hangs something quiet
    And queer—like a spell.

Beneath the arching sprays of bramble
    Small creatures make their holes;
Over the moss's close green velvet
    The stilted spider strolls.

The stalks of toadstools pale and slender
    That grow from that old log,
Bars they might be to imprison
    A prince turned to a frog.

There lives no mumbling witch nor wizard
    In this uncanny place,
Yet you might think you saw at twilight
    A little, crafty face.

# Cows

Half the time they munched the grass, and all the
    time they lay
Down in the water-meadows, the lazy month of May,
        A-chewing,
        A-mooing,
    To pass the hours away.

      'Nice weather,' said the brown cow.
      'Ah,' said the white.
      'Grass is very tasty.'
      'Grass is all right.'

Half the time they munched the grass, and all the
    time they lay
Down in the water-meadows, the lazy month of May,
        A-chewing,
        A-mooing,
    To pass the hours away.

      'Rain coming,' said the brown cow.
      'Ah,' said the white.
      'Flies is very tiresome.'
      'Flies bite.'

Half the time they munched the grass, and all the
    time they lay
Down in the water-meadows, the lazy month of May,
      A-chewing,
      A-mooing,
    To pass the hours away.

      'Time to go,' said the brown cow.
      'Ah,' said the white.
    'Nice chat.' 'Very pleasant.'
      'Night.' 'Night.'

Half the time they munched the grass, and all the
    time they lay
Down in the water-meadows, the lazy month of May,
      A-chewing,
      A-mooing,
    To pass the hours away.

# Elm Trees and

# Other People

# Trees in the Moonlight

Trees in the moonlight stand
  Still as a steeple,
And so quiet they seem like ghosts
  Of country people—

Dead farmers and their wives
  Of long, long ago,
Haunting the countryside
  They used to know;

Old gossips and talkers
  With tongues gone still;
Ploughmen rooted in the land
  They used to till;

Old carters and harvesters,
  Their wheels long rotten;
Old maids whose very names
  Time has forgotten.

Ghosts are they hereabouts;
  Them the moon sees,
Dark and still in the fields
  Like sleeping trees.

Long nights in autumn
  Hear them strain and cry,
Torn with a wordless sorrow
  As the gale sweeps by.

Spring makes fresh buds appear
   On the old boughs,
As if it could to their old wishes
   These ghosts arouse.

Trees in the summer night
   By moonlight linger on
So quiet they seem like ghosts
   Of people gone,

And it would be small wonder
   If at break of day
They heard the far-off cock-crow
   And fled away.

## *The Fiddler*

The blind man lifts his violin
And tucks it up right under his chin;
He saws with his fiddle-stick to and fro
And out comes the music sorrowful slow.

   Oh Shenandoah, it seems to say,
     Good-bye, you rolling river;
   To Londonderry I'm away
     Beside the weeping willow.

Ha'pennies and pennies he gets but few
As he fiddles his old tunes through and through;
But he nods and smiles as he scrapes away
And out comes the music sprightly and gay.

To the Irish washerwoman dancing a jig
In the land of Sweet Forever
Over the hills goes Tom with his pig,
And it's there we'll surely follow!


# Miss Wing

At the end of the street lives small Miss Wing,
A feathery, fluttery bird of a thing.
If you climb the street to the very top,
There you will see her fancy shop
With ribbons and buttons and frills and fluffs,
Pins and needles, purses and puffs,
Cosies and cushions and bits of chiffon,
And tiny hankies for ladies to sniff on,
And twists of silk and pieces of lace,
And odds and ends all over the place.
You push the door and the door-bell rings,
And the voice you hear is little Miss Wing's.
'Good-day, my dear, and how do you do?
Now tell me, what can I do for you?
Just half a second, please, dear Miss Gay—
As I was saying the other day—
Now what did I do with that so-and-so?
I'm sure I had it a moment ago—
As I was saying—why, yes, my dear—
A very nice day for the time of year—
Have you heard how poor Mrs Such-and-such?—
Oh, I hope I haven't charged too much;
That would never do—Now, what about pink?
It's nice for children, I always think—
Some buttons to go with a lavender frock?

Why now, I believe I'm out of stock—
Well, what about these? Oh, I never knew—
I'm ever so sorry—now what about blue?
Such a very nice woman—a flower for a hat?'
And so she goes on, with 'Fancy that!'
And 'You never can tell,' and 'Oh dear, no,'
And 'There now! it only goes to show.'
And on she goes like a hank of tape,
A reel of ribbon, a roll of crêpe,
Till you think her tongue will never stop.

And that's Miss Wing of the fancy shop.

# Mr Bellairs

In a huge hoary mansion
    Lives Mr Bellairs,
With four or five stories
    And hundreds of stairs.

The gates of his garden
    Are made of wrought iron.
From the top of each gatepost
    Glares down a great lion.

The trees in the garden
    Are ancient and stately,
And high in their branches
    Rooks mumble sedately.

The tails of the peacocks
  Sweep by on the grass;
The fish in the fishpond
  Gleam gold as they pass.

Superior tulips
  Adorn the parterres
In the exquisite garden
  Of Mr Bellairs.

But ah, the great mansion,
  The dark polished floors,
The marble, the mirrors,
  The gilt on the doors,

The bedrooms so blissful,
  The bathrooms so roomy,
The books in the library
  All learned and gloomy,

The cherubs on ceilings
  And stags on the wall,
The family portraits
  That line the great hall,

The carpets, the curtains,
  The fat chintzy chairs—
Oh, what a palazzo
  Has Mr Bellairs!

With such a great mansion
  And so many stairs
No wonder he's haughty
  And gives himself airs.

No wonder he's haughty
  With such an abode,
And his nose is quite straight
  Like the old Roman road.

# Mrs Golightly

Mrs Golightly's goloshes
    Are roomy and large;
Through water she slithers and sloshes,
    As safe as a barge.

When others at home must be stopping,
    To market she goes,
And returns later on with her shopping
    Tucked into her toes.

# Little Minnie Mystery

Little Minnie Mystery has packets and parcels
    All tied about with laces and strings,
And all full of scraps and patches and morsels
    And oddments and pieces and bits of things.

All tied about with strings and laces
    Are old Minnie Mystery's wonderful stores,
And she stows them away in all sorts of places—
    Cupboards and cases and chests of drawers.

All day long you will hear her caper
　　From attic to basement, up and down stairs,
Rummaging and rustling with tissue paper
　　And rattling keys and climbing on chairs.

What does she keep in her parcels and packets?—
　　Why, buckles and beads and knobs and handles,
Playing-cards, curtain-rings, loops, and lockets,
　　Letters and labels and Christmas-tree candles,

And a sea-shell box, and a peacock feather,
　　And a picture postcard from Tonypandy—
Everything neat and fastened together,
　　All that could possibly come in handy.

'Waste not, want not,' says Minnie Mystery.
　　'Everything's sure to come in some day.'
So, although she should live till the end of history,
　　Nothing she ever will throw away.

# Mrs Button

When Mrs Button, of a morning,
　　Comes creaking down the street,
You hear her old two black boots whisper
　　'Poor feet—poor feet—poor feet!'

When Mrs Button, every Monday,
　　Sweeps the chapel neat,
All down the long, hushed aisles they whisper
　　'Poor feet—poor feet—poor feet!'

Mrs Button after dinner
  (It is her Sunday treat)
Sits down and takes her two black boots off
  And rests her two poor feet.

# Mrs Gilfillan

When Mrs Gilfillan
  Is troubled with troubles,
She flies to the kitchen
  And sits blowing bubbles.
When Mrs Gilfillan
  Is worried by money,
When her feet are like lead
  And her head's feeling funny,
When there's too much to do,
  And the chimney is smoking,
And everything's awkward
  And wrong and provoking,
When the washing won't dry
  For the rain's never ending,
When the cupboards need cleaning
  And stockings want mending,
When the neighbours complain
  Of the noise of the cat,
And she ought to be looking
  For this and for that,
And never a line comes
  From her married daughter—
Then off to the kitchen
  With soap and warm water
Goes Mrs Gilfillan

And all her troubles;
  And she puffs them away
    In a great cloud of bubbles.
In joyful abandon
    She puffs them and blows them,
And all round about her
    In rapture she throws them;
When round, clear and shiny
    They hang in the air,
Away like a shadow
    Goes worry and care.

# *My Singing Aunt*

═══════════

The voice of magic melody
  With which my aunt delights me,
It drove my uncle to the grave
  And now his ghost affrights me.
This was the song she used to sing
  When I could scarcely prattle,
And as her top notes rose and fell
  They made the sideboard rattle:

'What makes a lady's cheeks so red,
  Her hair both long and wavy?
'Tis eating up her crusts of bread,
  Likewise her greens and gravy.
What makes the sailor rough and gay?
  What makes the ploughboy whistle?
'Tis eating salt-beef twice a day,
  And never mind the gristle.'

102

Thus sang my aunt in days gone by
    To soothe, caress, and calm me;
But what delighted me so much
    Drove her poor husband barmy.
So now when past the church I stray,
    'Tis not the night-wind moaning,
That chills my blood and stops my breath,
    But poor old uncle's groaning.

# Diddling

The people of Diddling
    Are never more than middling
For they can't abide either cold or heat.
    If the weather is damp,
    It gives them cramp,
And a touch of frost goes straight to their feet.

A thundery shower
    Turns everything sour,
And a dry spell ruins the farmers' crops,
    And a south-west wind
    Is nobody's friend
For it blows the smoke down the chimney-tops.

Says old Mrs Morley,
    'I'm middling poorly,
But thank you, I never was one to complain;
    For the cold in my nose
    As soon as it goes
I dursn't but say I may get it again.'

Old Grandfather Snell
Has never been well
Since he took to his crutches at seventy-three;
And the elder Miss Lake
Has a travelling ache
Which finds its way down from her neck to her knee.

The people of Diddling
Are never more than middling—
Not one but has headaches or palsy or gout.
But what they fear worst
Is a fine sunny burst,
For then there'll be nothing to grumble about.

## Poor Rumble

Pity poor Rumble: he is growing wheezy.
    At seventy-nine years old
His breath comes hard, and nothing comes too easy.
    He finds the evenings cold.

Pity poor Rumble: winter on his noddle
    Has laid its wisps of snow;
And though about the place he scarce can toddle,
    He likes to work, I know.

Pity poor Rumble: his last teeth are rotting
    Back in his square old head;
And yet, come Whitsuntide, you'll find him potting
    Down in his potting-shed.

Pity poor Rumble: since the time of Noah
 There was in all the county
For rose, or root, or greens no better grower—
 It was sheer bounty.

He was the champion for fruit or tatey;
 But Rumble's famous marrow,
So huge it was and more than common weighty,
 It almost split his barrow.

Of cat and dog he was the holy terror—
 None ever plagued him twice;
And if a slug walked on his lawn in error,
 His language was not nice.

Pity poor Rumble: now his strength is going.
 No more he'll cut up wood.
I wish I had some peaches of his growing;
 They were so very good.

Sing, birds of the air, for Martin Rumble, please.
 When he is gone away,
Who will grow strawberries for you, green peas,
 And currants on the spray?

# The Street

## Musician

# The Street Musician
### (based on the words of a song by Schubert)

With plaintive fluting, sad and slow,
    The old man by the roadside stands.
Who would have thought such notes could flow
    From such cracked lips and withered hands?

On shivering legs he stoops and sways,
    And not a passer stops to hark;
No penny cheers him as he plays;
    About his feet the mongrels bark.

But piping through the bitter weather,
    He lets the world go on its way.
Old piper! let us go together,
    And I will sing and you shall play.

# Fireworks

They rise like sudden fiery flowers
    That burst upon the night,
Then fall to earth in burning showers
    Of crimson, blue, and white.

Like buds too wonderful to name,
    Each miracle unfolds,
And catherine-wheels begin to flame
    Like whirling marigolds.

Rockets and Roman candles make
    An orchard of the sky,
Whence magic trees their petals shake
    Upon each gazing eye.


# The Statue

On a stone chair in the market-place
Sits a stone gentleman with a stone face.
He is great, he is good, he is old as old—
How many years I've not been told.
Great things he did a great while ago,
And what they were I do not know.
But solemn and sad is his great square face
As he sits high up on his square stone base.
Day after day he sits just so,
With some words in a foreign tongue below.
Whether the wind blows warm or cold,
His stone clothes alter never a fold.
One stone hand he rests on his knee;
With the other stone hand he points at me.
Oh, why does he look at me in just that way?
I'm afraid to go, and afraid to stay:
Stone gentleman, what have you got to say?

# The Piano

There is a lady who plays a piano;
    She lets me listen if I keep still.
I love to watch her twinkling fingers
    Fly up and down in scale or trill.

I love to hear the great chords crashing
    And making the huge black monster roar;
I love to hear the little chords falling
    Like sleepy waves on a summer shore.

Here comes an army with drums and trumpets,
    Now it's a battlefield, now it's a fire;
Now it's a waterfall boiling and bubbling,
    Now it's a bird singing higher and higher.

Now in the moonlight watch the trees bending,
    Water-nymphs rise from the bed of a stream;
Now in the garden the fountains are playing
    And in the sunshine flowers sway and dream.

Sometimes Harlequin comes with sweet Columbine,
    Sometimes I see deserts and twinkling stars,
The goose-girl, the fairies, a giant, a pygmy,
    And dark muffled strangers in foreign bazaars. . . .

All these I see when I hear that piano,
    All these and many things more do I see,
While over the keyboard the lady's hands travel,
    Yet nothing she sings, and no word says she.

# Rum Lane

Gusty and chill
  Blows the wind in Rum Lane,
And the spouts are a-spill
  With the fast-driving rain.

No footfall, no sound!
  Not a cat slithers by.
Men of sense, I'll be bound,
  Are at home in the dry.

Tall, dark, and narrow
  Are houses and shops—
Scarce room for a sparrow
  Between the roof-tops.

But oh! what a history
  Of rum and romance
Could be made from the mystery
  Of old Rum Lane once—

For this was the place
  Where they stowed silk apparel,
Old wine and old lace,
  And rum in the barrel!

Gusty and chill
  Blows the wind in Rum Lane,
And the spouts are a-spill
  With the fast-driving rain.

But no footfall, no tread,
  No step on the cobble
Will fright you in bed,
  You can sleep free of trouble;

For smuggling is over,
  And never again
Will any wild rover
  Be caught in Rum Lane.


# Uriconium

There was a man of Uriconium
Who played a primitive harmonium,
Inventing, to relieve his tedium,
Melodies high, low and medium,
And standing on his Roman cranium
Amidst a bed of wild geranium,
Better known as pelargonium,
Since with odium his harmonium
Was received in Uriconium.

# The Black Pebble

There went three children down to the shore,
  Down to the shore and back;
There was skipping Susan and bright-eyed Sam
  And little scowling Jack.

Susan found a white cockle-shell,
  The prettiest ever seen,
And Sam picked up a piece of glass
  Rounded and smooth and green.

But Jack found only a plain black pebble
  That lay by the rolling sea,
And that was all that ever he found;
  So back they went all three.

The cockle-shell they put on the table,
  The green glass on the shelf,
But the little black pebble that Jack had found,
  He kept it for himself.

# Pat's Fiddle

When Pat plays his fiddle
  In the great empty hall,
And the flame of each candle
  Is shiny and small,
        Then to hear the brave jingle,
        Oh, how my feet tingle
And how I do wish we could have a fine ball!

        Like a riddle, like a riddle
          Without any answer,
        Is a fiddle, sweet fiddle,
          With never a dancer.

Then out of the shadows
  And down the dark stairs
Come the ghosts of bright ladies
  And tall cavaliers.
        Oh, see with what pleasure
        They step out the measure!
His heart is as gay as the colour she wears.

        Like a riddle, like a riddle
          Without any answer,
        Is a fiddle, sweet fiddle,
          With never a dancer.

I hear from each partner
Who passes me by
The faintest of whispers,
The ghost of a sigh.
For there'll be no hiding
The pain of dividing
When the strains of the fiddle shall falter and die.

Like a riddle, like a riddle
Without any answer,
Is a fiddle, sweet fiddle,
With never a dancer.

So play no more, Paddy,
Of fiddlers the best.
The spent candles bid us
Good-night and good rest.
When music entrancing
Sets both my feet dancing,
There's something inside me that can't be expressed.
Now rest your old fingers
While darkness yet lingers,
For yonder has vanished the last ghostly guest.

# Boating

Gently the river bore us
  Beneath the morning sky,
Singing, singing, singing
Its reedy, quiet tune
  As we went floating by;
And all that afternoon
  In our small boat we lay
Rocking, rocking, rocking
  Under the willows grey.
When into bed that evening
  I climbed, it seemed a boat
Was softly rocking, rocking,
Rocking me to sleep,
  And I was still afloat.
I heard the grey leaves weep
  And whisper round my bed,
The river singing, singing,
  Singing through my head.

# Myths and

# Wonders

# Giant Thunder

Giant Thunder, striding home,
Wonders if his supper's done.

'Hag wife, hag wife, bring me my bones!'
'They are not done,' the old hag moans.

'Not done? not done?' the giant roars
And heaves his old wife out of doors.

Cries he, 'I'll have them, cooked or not!'
But overturns the cooking-pot.

He flings the burning coals about;
See how the lightning flashes out!

Upon the gale the old hag rides,
The cloudy moon for terror hides.

All the world with thunder quakes;
Forest shudders, mountain shakes;
From the cloud the rainstorm breaks;
Village ponds are turned to lakes;
Every living creature wakes.

Hungry Giant, lie you still!
Stamp no more from hill to hill—
Tomorrow you shall have your fill.

# The Magic Seeds

There was an old woman who sowed a corn seed,
And from it there sprouted a tall yellow weed.
She planted the seeds of the tall yellow flower,
And up sprang a blue one in less than an hour,
The seed of the blue one she sowed in a bed,
And up sprang a tall tree with blossoms of red.
And high in the treetop there sang a white bird,
And his song was the sweetest that ever was heard.
The people they came from far and from near,
The song of the little white bird for to hear.

# Pluto and Proserpine

Said Pluto the King
   To Princess Proserpine,
'I will give you a marriage ring
   If you will be my Queen.'

Said she, 'What flowers spring
   Underneath your sun?'
Said he, 'Where I am King
   Flowers there are none.'

'And do the gay birds sing
    In your country?' said she.
'You shall hear where I am King
    None but the owl,' said he.

'Do the people laugh and play?'
    Asked Princess Proserpine.
'Are the children happy as day
    In the meadows soft and green?'

Said the King, 'There are no meadows
    In the country where I reign.
My people are all shadows;
    They will not laugh again.

'Sunshine you shall not see
    In the Kingdom of the Dead:
Queen of that kingdom you shall be,
    If you and I are wed.'

Said she, 'I am tired of flowers
    And the gay birds' song;
I am tired of the sunny hours
    In the meadows day long.

'But the dark I will not fear,
    And you and I will wed;
And the sad ones I will cheer
    In the grey land of the dead.'

So Pluto the King
    Took the Princess by the hand,
And with the marriage ring
    Made her Queen in his land.

# Troy

Priam is the king of ashes.
   Heroes die and gods lament.
Round his head his kingdom crashes.
   Now the ten years' war is spent.

Night in flames and no man sleeping,
   Trumpets' scream across the plains,
Charging horsemen, women weeping—
   These are all that now remains:

These and not the shouts of gladness,
   Not the victors' face of joy,
These I see and hear in sadness
   When I think of fallen Troy.

# The Moonlit Stream

A stream far off beneath the moon
   Flowed silver-bright and thin,
Winding its way like some slow tune
   Played on a violin.

The valley trees were hushed and still;
    The sky was pearly grey;
The moonlight slept upon the hill—
    As white as snow it lay.

Then softly from a ruined tower
    That rose beside the stream
A bell chimed out the midnight hour;
    And then—Oh, did I dream?—

Then all at once a long, black boat
    With neither sail nor oars
Down that bright stream began to float
    Between its shadowy shores.

No passenger nor steersman stirred
    On that enchanted thing;
But faint, unearthly-sweet, I heard
    A choir of voices sing.

It moved mysterious and serene,
    A sable-feathered swan;
It seemed the soul of some sad queen
    Was borne to Avalon.

So in my thoughts that shadowy boat
    Will sail the moonlit river,
And faintly I shall hear the note
    Of that sad choir for ever.

## Bobadil

Far from far
  Lives Bobadil
In a tall house
  On a tall hill.

Out from the high
  Top window-sill
On a clear night
  Leans Bobadil

To touch the moon,
  To catch a star,
To keep in her tall house
  Far from far.


## The Three Singing Birds

The King walked in his garden green,
  Where grew a marvellous tree;
And out of its leaves came singing birds
  By one, and two, and three.

The first bird had wings of white,
  The second had wings of gold,
The third had wings of deepest blue
  Most beauteous to behold.

The white bird flew to the northern land,
  The gold bird flew to the west,
The blue bird flew to the cold, cold south
  Where never bird might nest.

The King waited a twelvemonth long,
  Till back the three birds flew,
They lighted down upon the tree,
  The white, the gold, and the blue.

The white bird brought a pearly seed
  And gave it to the King;
The gold bird from out of the west
  He brought a golden ring.

The third bird with feathers blue
  Who came from the far cold south,
A twisted sea-shell smooth and grey
  He carried in his mouth.

The King planted the pearly seed
  Down in his garden green,
And up there sprang a pearl-white maid,
  The fairest ever seen.

She looked at the King and knelt her down
  All under the magic tree,
She smiled at him with her red lips
  But not a word said she.

123

Instead she took the grey sea-shell
    And held it to his ear,
She pressed it close and soon the King
    A strange, sweet song did hear.

He raised the fair maid by the hand
    Until she stood at his side;
Then he gave her the golden ring
    And took her for his bride.

And at their window sang the birds,
    They sang the whole night through,
Then off they went at break of day,
    The white, the gold, and the blue.

# Kingdom Cove

When I went down to Kingdom Cove,
The cliffs were brown, the sea was mauve.
Shadows of rocks on the clifftops lay
As the sunset flamed across the bay.
I saw three starfish upon the shore
And up in the sky was one fish more.
Birds on the tumbling waters cried
'Ship's away with the morning tide!'
But the man in the lighthouse called to me,
'Don't go crossing the tumbling sea!'
And I saw his telescope up to his eye
Gazing out to the sunset sky.
So I shouted out, 'But the night is black:
If I don't go on, I can't go back!'

And then a great storm cracked the sky
And a giant sea-bird scouted by,
He carried me off on his cloudy track
And set me down on a dolphin's back.
There is an island out to sea,
Where tall trees wait to sing for me;
Sing they will in the autumn gale,
And there on the dolphin's back I'll sail.
In Kingdom Cove my father stands,
Shading his eyes with two brown hands,
And three red starfish crumble away
And the land-breeze blows them across the bay.

# The Horn

'Oh, hear you a horn, mother, behind the hill?
My body's blood runs bitter and chill.
The seven long years have passed, mother, passed,
And here comes my rider at last, at last.
I hear his horse now, and soon I must go.
How dark is the night, mother, cold the winds blow.
How fierce the hurricane over the deep sea!
For a seven years' promise he comes to take me.'

'Stay at home, daughter, stay here and hide.
I will say you have gone, I will tell him you died.
I am lonely without you, your father is old;
Warm is our hearth, daughter, but the world is cold.'

'Oh mother, oh mother, you must not talk so.
In faith I promised, and for faith I must go,
For if that old promise I should not keep,
For seven long years, mother, I would not sleep.

Seven years my blood would run bitter and chill
To hear that sad horn, mother, behind the hill.
My body once frozen by such a shame
Would never be warmed, mother, at your hearth's
    flame.
But round my true heart shall the arms of the storm
For ever be folded, protecting and warm.'

# Time to go

# Home

# Time to go Home

Time to go home!
　Says the great steeple clock.
Time to go home!
　Says the gold weathercock.
Down sinks the sun
　In the valley to sleep;
Lost are the orchards
　In blue shadows deep.
Soft falls the dew
　On cornfield and grass;
Through the dark trees
　The evening airs pass:
Time to go home,
　They murmur and say;
Birds to their homes
　Have all flown away.
Nothing shines now
　But the gold weathercock.
Time to go home!
　Says the great steeple clock.

# Prefabulous Animiles

# Let No One Suppose

Let no one suppose
That the creatures he knows—
The robin, the rat,
The cat on the mat,
The toad in his hole,
The vole and the mole,
The hog and the dog,

The fat, freckled frog,
The fish in the seas
And the birds in the trees,
The beasts in the Zoo,
The paunched kangaroo,
The swan on the lake,
The serpent or snake,
The ant, the ant-eater,
The chimp and the cheetah—
Let no one suppose that creatures like those
Are ALL that the Animal Kingdom can show:
                                        NO!

When the woods rumble low
And storm-clouds ride by in the purplish sky,
At the corners of dreams,
Round the edges of sleep,
There's a something that *seems* to be going to creep,
To crawl or to climb, to lumber or leap
Round the corners of dreams and the edges of sleep.
You cannot be sure that you fastened the door,
You cannot be certain that under the curtain
There isn't a tail or a paw or a claw.
And what makes you wonder is never the thunder
Nor wind in the chimney nor rain on the tiles,
It *must be—*
        PREFABULOUS ANIMILES!

So if any suppose
That the creatures he knows
In pond or in park,
By daylight and dark,
Are all that the Animal Kingdom contains,
Then some day he'll see them lurking in lanes,
Or breaking down hedges and fences and stiles—
He'll *see* the Prefabulous Animiles.

# The Hippocrump

Along the valley of the Ump
Gallops the fearful Hippocrump.
His hide is leathery and thick;
His eyelids open with a *Click!*
His mouth he closes with a *Clack!*
He has three humps upon his back;
On each of these there grows a score
Of horny spikes, and sometimes more.
His hair is curly, thick and brown;
Beneath his chin a beard hangs down.
He has eight feet with hideous claws;
His neck is long—and O his jaws!
The boldest falters in his track
To hear those hundred teeth go *Clack!*
The Hippocrump is fierce indeed,
But if he eats the baneful weed
That grows beside the Purple Lake,
His hundred teeth begin to ache.

Then how the creature stamps and roars
Along the Ump's resounding shores!
The drowsy cattle faint with fright;
The birds fall flat, the fish turn white.
Even the rocks begin to shake;
The children in their beds awake;
The old ones quiver, quail, and quake.
'Alas!' they cry. 'Make no mistake,
It is *Himself*—he's got the Ache
From eating by the Purple Lake!'
Some say, 'It is *Old You-know-who*—
He's in a rage: what *shall* we do?'
'Lock up the barns, protect the stores,
Bring all the pigs and sheep indoors!'

They call upon their god, Agw-ump
To save them from the Hippocrump.
'What's that I hear go hop-skip-jump?
He's coming! Stand aside there!' *Bump!*
*Lump-lump!*—'He's on the bridge now!'—*Lump!*
'I hear his tail'—*ker-flump, ker-flump!*
'I see the prickles on his hump!
It *is*, it IS—the Hippocrump!
Defend us now, O Great Agw-ump!'

Thus prayed the dwellers by the Ump.
Their prayer was heard. A broken stump
Caught the intruder in the rump.
He slipped into the foaming river,
Whose icy water quenched his fever,
Then while the creature floundering lay,
The timid people ran away;
And when the morrow dawned serene
The Hippocrump was no more seen.
Glad hymns of joy the people raised:
'For ever Great Agw-ump be praised!'

# The Nimp

Behold the supercilious Nimp,
   The most select of creatures.
He has two flippers, long and limp,
   Snub nose, and other features.

If bird or beast approach too near,
   He looks at it with hauteur,
Then shambles sadly to the mere
   And dives into the water.

But if the fishes swim too close,
   With air serene and bland
And blowing proudly through his nose
   He paddles back to land.

## The Doze

Through Dangly Woods the aimless Doze
A-dripping and a-dribbling goes.
His company no beast enjoys.
He makes a sort of hopeless noise
Between a snuffle and a snort.
His hair is neither long nor short;
His tail gets caught on briars and bushes,
As through the undergrowth he pushes.
His ears are big, but not much use.
He lives on blackberries and juice
And anything that he can get.
His feet are clumsy, wide and wet,
Slip-slopping through the bog and heather
All in the wild and weepy weather.
His young are many, and maltreat him;
But only hungry creatures eat him.
He pokes about in mossy holes,
Disturbing sleepless mice and moles,
And what he wants he never knows—
The damp, despised, and aimless Doze.

# The Bisk

In Waikee-waik
Beside the Lake
Unseen by any stranger,
The little Bisk
Delights to frisk,
Oblivious of all danger.

At break of day
She seeks her prey
Along the Mukmuk River;
And when she sings,
Her spotted wings
Begin to quake and quiver.

The courting male
Has for a tail
One tall luxuriant feather,
With which displayed
He makes a shade
To keep her from the weather.

In summer days
One egg she lays
And finds a secret nook for it;
But she the spot
Remembers not,
So sends her mate to look for it.

By Mukmuk's shore
  She gathers store
Of berries each September,
  But where she puts
  Her nuts and fruits
She never *can* remember.

  O gaily, gaily,
  Ten times daily
She flits on careless wing!
  Speak no harsh word
  Of this small bird,
Who only lives to sing.

# The Catipoce

'O Harry, Harry! hold me close—
　　I fear some animile.
It is the horny Catipoce
　　With her outrageous smile!'

Thus spoke the maiden in alarm;
　　She had good cause to fear:
The Catipoce can do great harm,
　　If any come too near.

Despite her looks, do not presume
　　The creature's ways are mild;
For many have gone mad on whom
　　The Catipoce has smiled.

She lurks in woods at close of day
　　Among the toadstools soft,
Or sprawls on musty sacks and hay
　　In cellar, barn, or loft.

Behind neglected rubbish-dumps
　　At dusk your blood will freeze
Only to glimpse her horny humps
　　And hear her fatal sneeze.

Run, run! adventurous boy or girl—
　　Run home, and do not pause
To feel her breath around you curl,
　　And tempt her carrion claws.

Avoid her face: for underneath
   That gentle, fond grimace
Lie four-and-forty crooked teeth—
   My dears, avoid her face!

'O Harry, Harry! hold me close,
   And hold me close a while;
It is the odious Catipoce
   With her devouring smile!'

# The Chickamungus

All in the groves of dragon-fungus
Lives the mysterious Chickamungus.
The people who inhabit there
Have never yet found out his lair;
And if by chance they did, no doubt
The Chickamungus would be out.
For he is seldom found at home;
He likes to rove, he likes to roam.
He never sleeps but what he snores,
He never barks but what he roars,
He never creeps but what he walks,
He never climbs but what he stalks,
He never trots but what he hobbles,
He never stands but what he wobbles,
He never runs but what he skims,
He never flies but what he swims,
At tom-tom time he romps and roves
Among the odorous dragon-groves.
He lives on half-grown formicoots
And other sorts of roots and shoots.
He has been seen at rest among
His multitudinivorous young;
And travellers returning late
Have heard him crying for his mate.
His tracks have been identified,
Straying a bit from side to side,
Across the desert plains of Quunce.
A little girl observed him once,
But could not say what she had seen,

So unobservant had she been.
Her evidence is inconclusive,
And so the beast remains elusive.
A naturalist who found his den
Was never after seen again.
Thus we must leave the Chickamungus
At large amidst the dragon-fungus.

# The Nonny

The Nonny-bird I love particularly;
   All day she chirps her joysome odes.
She rises perpendicularly,
   And if she goes too far, explodes.

# The Osc

This is the superfluminous Osc,
  A mild and serious liver;
He skims each day from dawn till dusk
  The surface of the river.

For gentleness he is the best
  Of all amphibious creatures;
His wide and wondering eyes suggest
  An old, forgotten teacher's.

In, out—in, out—he weaves his way
  Along the limpid shallows,
Or upside-down hangs half a day
  Amidst the ruminous sallows.

In mating time he bleats and sings
  To entertain his bride,
He wiggles both his graceful wings
  And jumps from side to side.

No hawk invades his harmless path,
  No boar with cruel tusk,
No alligator mad with wrath
  Attacks the little Osc.

He lives on fluff and water-weed
  And bits of this and that
Which other creatures do not need.
  His ears are round and flat.

Thus, free from terror, want and sin,
   Proceeds from dusk to dusk
Out, in—out, in—with careless fin
   The superfluminous Osc.

# The Snyke

Deep in the Jungles of Jam-kaïk
Wanders the forty-leggèd Snyke,
And I can tell you what he's like
   For I have seen him oft.
His eyes are like two coals afire;
His hair is harsh as copper wire;
His jaws are dark, and deep, and dire;
   His tread is smooth and soft.

Where grows the giant scented cress
In that close-coiling wilderness
Amid the jungle silences
    Where nights are thick and sweet,
The watch-dogs scarcely dare to bark;
The people tremble as they hark
To hear *pad-padding* through the dark
    Those forty fearful feet.

'The Snyke! It is the Snyke!' they wail.
To hear that slithery, scratchy tail
The strongest feel their courage fail
    And dither at the knees.
He overturns their cooking-pots;
He ties the women's hair in knots;
He brings their children out in spots,
    And blights the orchard trees.

So then with arrow, spear and bow
About the woods the warriors go,
Vowing vengeance, crying *Woe*
    Upon the dreadful Snyke.
There is a huge and special pot
By servants kept for ever hot,
In which they'll stew, when they have got,
    The Terror of Jam-kaïk.

They'll cut him up in little slices,
Flavour him well with salt and spices,
Torment him first with slow devices,
    Ingenious and sure.
Meanwhile, they have not got him yet;
He lives to make the boldest sweat,
To scare the maids, and overset
    The stewpots of the poor.

# The Amperzand

This is the common Amperzand.
His graceful lines observe
When wiggling through the desert sand
    With complicated curve.
There is no man in India's land
    Who has sufficient nerve
To tame the sinuous Amperzand
    Some useful end to serve.
Bring me my oboe from the shelf—
*I'll* make the creature stir himself!

# The Snitterjipe

In mellow orchards, rich and ripe,
Is found the luminous Snitterjipe.
Bad boys who climb the bulging trees
Feel his sharp breath about their knees;
His trembling whiskers tickle so,
They squeak and squeal till they let go.
They hear his far-from-friendly bark;
They see his eyeballs in the dark
Shining and shifting in their sockets
As round and big as pears in pockets.
They feel his hot and wrinkly hide;
They see his nostrils flaming wide,
His tapering teeth, his jutting jaws,
His tongue, his tail, his twenty claws.
His hairy shadow in the moon,
It makes them sweat, it makes them swoon;
And as they climb the orchard wall,
They let their pilfered pippins fall.
The Snitterjipe suspends pursuit
And falls upon the fallen fruit;
And while they flee the monster fierce,
Apples, not boys, his talons pierce.
With thumping hearts they hear him munch—
Six apples at a time he'll crunch.
At length he falls asleep, and they
On tiptoe take their homeward way.

But long before the blackbirds pipe
To welcome day, the Snitterjipe
Has fled afar, and on the green
Only his fearsome prints are seen.

# The Blether

=====

'Up, up, my sons, my daughter dear—
    Go forth this day together!
To horse, to horse! take hound and horn
    And hunt the baneful Blether.

'Last night I felt his baneful breath
    Upon my forehead chill.
These spots so red upon my head
    I fear may work me ill.'

Thus groaning on his bed of pain,
    We heard the old man sigh:
'Unless you kill the fexious beast,
    Tomorrow I shall die!'

The dawn was cold, the stars were few,
    And furious was the weather,
When one and all we started out
    To track the noisome Blether.

'Avoid his eye, avoid his breath,
    Avoid his crackling teeth!
Take care, take care! his silky hair
    Has prickles underneath.'

Full swift I rode the old white horse,
    My sister rode the grey.
Upon the backs of four great blacks
    My brothers rode that day.

We hunted high, we hunted low,
　　We sought through heath and heather.
Through sun and shade the fox-hounds bayed—
　　They smelt the noxious Blether.

We hunted high, we hunted low;
　　My sister sighed full sore.
My brother Richard's horse fell lame,
　　And he could ride no more.

The Gargle and the Gallimo
　　We passed with lightsome bounds;
But there beneath the boiling tide
　　We lost our swiftest hounds.

Right soon we came to Woeful Woods,
　　And there the Beast we spied.
'Press on, press on!' cried Brother John.
　　'I can no further ride.'

We heard his tread, we saw his tail,
　　We smelt his fexious breath;
And that foul cry that smote the sky,
　　It was the cry of death!

But as we flashed through Crocus Copse,
　　Right ruminous waxed the weather.
Up, up the hill we followed still
　　The thrice-accursèd Blether.

The thunderbolts came crashing down,
　　The thunder groaned full sore.
'Now strike me dead!' cried Brother Ned,
　　'For I can ride no more.

'But ride ye on, my comrades dear,
　　Though I no more can ride.
Beware his teeth, his noisome breath,
　　The prickles in his hide.'

We hunted high, we hunted low,
　　We rode through flood and fell;
Across the snow we chased the foe,
　　We knew his marks full well.

Across the snow we chased the foe,
　　We knew his marks full well;
On Tangley Top we saw him stop
　　And breathe his frightful spell.

Three times the monster breathed his spell
　　Across the deathly snow.
My brother Guy made fearful cry:
　　'I can no longer go!'

Full swift I spurred the milk-white steed,
   My sister spurred the grey.
Past moor and mountain, tower and hall,
   We sped that direful day.

We hunted high, we hunted low,
   We rode o'er hill and dale.
'Now ever alack, my sister dear,
   Why lookest thou so pale?'

'Alack, alack, my brother dear,
   I fear my horse will fall.'
'Now what is that by yonder tree?
It is, it is—deny not me!
   It is my father's hall.'

'And what is that in yonder field
   Stone-dead amidst the heather?'
'Deny me not! It is, I wot,
   It is the baneful Blether!'

My father he has risen up,
   Set forth a joyful feast.
'The baneful Blether he is dead;
No more, my children, shall we dread
   The thrice-accursèd Beast!'

# Ragged
# Robin

# Ragged Robin

Robin was a king of men,
A king of far renown,
But then he fell on evil days
And lost his royal crown.
Ragged Robin he was called;
He lived in ragged times,
And so to earn his livelihood
He took to making rhymes.

A score or so of ragged rhymes
He made—some good, some bad;
He sang them up and down the lanes
Till people called him mad.

They listened for Mad Robin's songs
Through all the countryside,
And when they heard his voice no more
They guessed that he had died.

Now Ragged Robin was not dead
But changed into a bird,
And every year on tile and tree
His piping voice is heard.
His breast is clad with scarlet red,
His cloak and hood are brown;
And once more he is Winter's king
Although he wears no crown.

Cold are the skies where Robin reigns,
And evergreen his throne.
He whistles to defy the wind;
His tunes are all his own.
But here within this book are set
Some of the ragged rhymes
Mad Robin by the hedgerows sang
In far-off ragged times.

# *Twenty-six Letters*

Twenty-six cards in half a pack;
Twenty-six weeks in half a year;
Twenty-six letters dressed in black
In all the words you ever will hear.

In 'King', 'Queen', 'Ace', and 'Jack',
In 'London', 'lucky', 'lone', and 'lack',
'January', 'April', 'fortify', 'fix',
You'll never find more than twenty-six.

Think of the beautiful things you see
On mountain, riverside, meadow and tree.
How many their names are, but how small
The twenty-six letters that spell them all.

# A
## Avalon

In Avalon lies Arthur yonder;
Over his head the planets wander.
   A great King
   And a great King was he.

By his side sleeps Guinevere;
Of ladies she had no peer.
   A fair Queen
   And a fair Queen was she.

At midnight comes Jack the Knave
By moonlight to rob their grave.
   A false boy
   And a false boy is he.

Jewels he takes, and rings,
The gift of nobles and kings—
   Bright things,
   O bright things to see!

On harvest-field and town
The moon and stars look down.
Centuries without number
King and Queen are a-slumber.
   Long have they lain.
In time they will rise again
And all false knaves be slain.
Once more Arthur shall reign.
   A great King
   And a great King is he.

# B
## Brand the Blacksmith

Brand the Blacksmith with his hard hammer
Beats out shoes for the hooves of horses.
Bagot the Boy works at the bellows
To make fine mounts for the King's forces.

Better the music than bell or bugle
When 'Huff!' go the bellows and 'Ding!' goes the
  hammer.
'Better this work by far,' says Bagot,
'Than banging of school bell and grinding at grammar.'

# C
## *Castles and Candlelight*

Castles and candlelight
Are courtly things.
Turreted high
For the children of Kings
Stands the fair castle
Over the strand,
And there with a candle
In her thin hand,
With tunes in her ears
And gold on her head
Climbs the sad Princess
Upstairs to bed.

Castles and candlelight
Are cruel things,
For castles have dungeons,
And moths have wings.
Woe to the shepherd-boy
Who in darkness lies,
For viewing the Princess
With love in his eyes.
Ah, the poor shepherd-boy—
How long will it be
Before the proud King
Will let him go free?

# D
## The Song of D

Who will sing me the song of D?
How many dancers can you see?
Dinah, Deborah, Duncan, Dick,
And Dan with his fiddle and fiddling stick.
  Sing it low, sing it high,
Till the glory shines in the western sky.

Who will sing me the song of D?
How many cities can you see?
From Dublin Town we'll all jump over
To Dartmouth, Darlington, Deal and Dover.
  Sing it low, sing it high,
Till the glory shines in the western sky.

Who will sing me the song of D?
How many flowers can you see?
Daffodil, dahlia, daisy, dock,
Dandelion seed to make a clock.
  Sing it low, sing it high,
Till the glory shines in the western sky.

Who will sing me the song of D?
How many creatures can you see?
Dodo, dromedary, dingo, duck,
And the direful Dragon who brings bad luck.
  Sing it low, sing it high,
Till the glory shines in the western sky.

Who will sing me the song of D?
How many people can you see?
Doctor, dowager, dustman, duke—
If you want any more you must go and look.
　　Sing it low, sing it high,
Till the glory shines in the western sky.


# E
## Egg to Eat

Early this morning when earth was empty
I went to the farmyard to fetch me an egg.
I spoke to the pullets who strolled about scratching
And the proud feathered cock who stood on one leg.

'Not an egg! Not an egg!' they all said together.
'We haven't been given any corn for two days.'
So I went to the merchant who lives by the market,
And I asked him to give me some barley and maize.

'Not a grain! Not a grain!' was the corn-merchant's
　　answer.
'I need a new wheel for to fix on my cart.'
So I said to the wheelwright, 'Please give me a wheel, sir,
For without it the corn-merchant's wagon won't start.'

'Not a wheel, not a wheel can I make!' said the
　　wheelwright.
'If you bring a new hammer, why then I will try.'
So I searched up and down, but I couldn't find a hammer,
And I went to the forest to sit down and cry.

There I met an old wife and asked her politely,
'Oh madam, can you lend me a hammer, I beg?'
'Why no,' said the wife, 'for I haven't got a hammer,
But if it will help you, I will give you an egg.'

So she gave me an egg, and I said to her, 'Madam,
This surely must be the best egg ever born.'
'So it is,' said the wife. 'If you want the best eggs,
You must always give your laying birds plenty of corn.'

# F
## Flirt and Frost

Flowers and Frost

Flowers are yellow
And flowers are red;
Frost is white
As an old man's head.
Daffodil, foxglove,
Rose, sweet pea—
Flowers and frost
Can never agree.
Flowers will wither
And summer's lost
When over the mountain
Comes King Frost.

White are the fields
Where King Frost reigns;
And the ferns he draws
On window-panes,
White and stiff
Are their curling fronds.

White are the hedges
And stiff are the ponds.
So cruel and hard
Is winter's King,
With his icy breath
On everything.

Then up comes the sun;
Down fall the showers.
Welcome to spring
And her yellow flowers!
So sing the birds
On the budding tree,
For frost and flowers
Can never agree;
And welcome, sunshine,
That we may say
The old cruel King
Is driven away.

# G
# Green Grass

Green grass is all I hear
And grass is all I see
When through tall fields I wander
Swish-swishing to the knee.

Grass is short on the high heath
And long on the hillside.
There's where the rabbits burrow,
And here's where I hide.

The hillside is my castle,
Its walls are the tall grass;
Over them I peer and pry
To see the people pass.

Long and far I send my gaze
Over the valleys low.
There I can see but do not hear
The wagons lumbering slow.

Horseman, footman, shepherd, dog—
Here in my castle green
I see them move through vale and village,
I see but am not seen.

Green grasses whispering round me,
All in the summer fine,
Tell me your secrets, meadow grasses,
And I will tell you mine.

# H
## *Heroes on Horseback*

Heroes on horseback
Hunt in their hundreds,
Leaving their halls
In the hurry of morn.
High on the hilltop
Is heard the thunder
Of hooves, and the hue
Of hound and horn.

Here in their homesteads
Hover the housewives,
Baking and brewing
Or busy with brush.
Gaily they gossip
And stitch for the children;
For hunting and harrying
They care not a rush.

High in the heavens
The hooked moon hangs.
Home come the hunters
Hungry as hawks.
Never a hare
Has Harry the Huntsman
Caught the whole day,
But hark how he talks!

'Hunters on horseback
Are braggers and boasters!'
So say the housewives
Who give them their stew.
'Without us women
To work and wait on them
What would these heroes,
Our husbands, do?'

# I
# Islands

I, with my mind's eye, see
Islands and indies fair and free,
Fair and far in the coral sea.

Out of the sea rise palmy shores;
Out of the shore rise plumy trees;
Out of each tree a feathered bird
Sings with a voice like which
    no voice was ever heard,
And palm and plume and feather
Blend and bloom together
In colours like the green
    of summer weather.

And in this island scene
There is no clash nor quarrel;
Here the seas wash
In shining fields of coral
Indies and isles that lie
Deep in my mind's eye.

# J
## *Jargon*

Jerusalem, Joppa, Jericho—
These are the cities of long ago.

Jasper, jacinth, jet and jade—
Of such are jewels for ladies made.

Juniper's green and jasmine's white,
Sweet jonquil is spring's delight.

Joseph, Jeremy, Jennifer, James,
Julian, Juliet—just names.

January, July and June—
Birthday late or birthday soon.

Jacket, jersey, jerkin, jeans—
What's the wear for sweet sixteens?

Jaguar, jackal, jumbo, jay—
Came to dinner but couldn't stay.

Jellies, junkets, jumbals, jam—
Mix them up for sweet-toothed Sam.

To jig, to jaunt, to jostle, to jest—
These are the things that Jack loves best.

Jazz, jamboree, jubilee, joke—
The jolliest words you ever spoke.

From A to Z and Z to A
The joyfullest letter of all is J.

# K
## Kay

Kay, Kay,
Good Sir Kay,
Lock the gate
Till dawn of day,
So to keep bad men away.

This is the Keep,
And this is the key.
Who keeps the key
Of the Keep?
              Sir Kay.

Kay, Kay,
Good Sir Kay,
Lock the gate
Till dawn of day.

The bell has rung
To evensong.
The priest has blessed
The kneeling throng.
In bower and hall
To bed have gone
Knights and squires
All and one,
Lords and ladies
One and all,
Groom in kitchen,
Steed in stall.

Kay, Kay,
Good Sir Kay,
Lock the gate
Till dawn of day.
On shield and scabbard
Starlight falls,
Stalk the watchmen
Along the walls.
From hazel thicket
The screech-owl calls.
By the dying fire
The boarhounds sleep.
Sir Kay, Sir Kay,
Lock fast the keep.

This is the Keep,
And this is the key.
Who keeps the key
Of the Keep?
                Sir Kay.

Kay, Kay,
Good Sir Kay,
Lock the gate
Till dawn of day,
So to keep bad men away.

It is late, late.
Lock fast the gate.


# L
## *Long*

A short word and a short word is 'long',
So let's have a short, not a long song.

'Long was my beard,' said the sailor,
  'Before we reached port.'
'Long are my dreams,' said the old man,
  'But memory's short.'
'Long are all days,' said the children,
  'With few of them gone.'
'Long are all lanes,' said the wanderer,
  'Leading me on.'

A short word and a short word is 'long',
So let's have a short, not a long song.

171

The sailor mended his tackle
  And searched for a breeze.
The old man thought of a voyage
  To unmapped seas.
The children, weary of playing,
  Came from the green;
The wanderer sighed for a home
  He had never seen.

A short word and a short word is 'long',
So that was a short, not a long song.

# M
## Moths and Moonshine

Moths and moonshine mean to me
Magic—madness—mystery.

Witches dancing weird and wild
Mischief make for man and child.

Owls screech from woodland shades,
Moths glide through moonlit glades,

Moving in dark and secret wise
Like a plotter in disguise.

Moths and moonshine mean to me
Magic—madness—mystery.

# N
## Noah

Noah was an Admiral;
Never a one but he
Sailed for forty days and nights
With wife and children three
On such a mighty sea.

Under his tempest-battered deck
This Admiral had a zoo;
And all the creatures in the world,
He kept them, two by two—
Ant, hippo, kangaroo,

And every other beast beside,
Of every mould and make.
When tempests howled and thunder growled
How they did cower and quake
To feel the vessel shake!

But Noah was a Carpenter
Had made his ship so sound
That not a soul of crew or zoo
In all that time was drowned
Before they reached dry ground.

So Admiral, Keeper, Carpenter—
Now should *you* put to sea
In such a flood, it would be good
If one of these you be,
But better still—all three!

# O
## *O Nay!*

'O nay! O nay! O nay!'
  I heard the crier call.
'There is no news today—
  No news, no news at all.

'No cow has gone astray!'
  I heard the crier call.
'No foe is on the way!
  There is no news at all.

'The Mayor has gone away.
  Good people, one and all,
Are now on holiday,'
  I heard the crier call.

'O nay! O nay! O nay!'
  I heard the crier cry.
'No folks in town do stay—
  Methinks no more will I!'

# P
## Paper

Paper makes a picture-book;
Paper and a pin
Make a coloured parcel
To wrap a present in.

Paper makes a letter
That makes a lady sad;
And sometimes it makes money
To make a poor man glad.

Paper, paper, paper
Makes a lawyer's clerk
Scribble, scratch and scribble
From morn till dead of dark.

Paper makes a dunce's cap;
Paper makes a kite.
I watch it rise upon the wind
And vanish out of sight.

Paper makes all shapes of things;
But best of all to me,
A paper boat upon the stream
Goes bobbing off to sea.

# Q
## *Quiet*

Of all creatures
   Quiet is the shyest;
She has her finger to her lips.
She loves not cities
   but a mountain lakeside
Where peaceful water laps.

At nesting-time
   to see the mother blackbird
Quiet on tiptoe creeps;
And in the kitchen
   with scarce a blink she watches
The mice come out for scraps.

In fairgrounds
   or by the August seaside
Quiet will not stop;
But walks in winter
   on snow fresh-fallen
With light and muffled step.

She loves the fireside
   when the guests have gone,
And downward the ember slips;
Beside the cot she lingers
   hardly breathing
Because the baby sleeps.

# R
## Rain

═══════════

Rain and rain is all I see
Falling on roof and stone and tree,
And all I hear is rain and rain
Hush-hushing on lawn and lane.

Moor and meadow, fern and flower
Drink the raindrops, hour by hour.
How sparkling are the ivy leaves
That catch the drops from farmhouse eaves!

When in my attic bed I lie
I hear it fall from the cloudy sky,
Hush-hushing all around
With its low and lulling sound.

Then in the light of morning clear
How new and green all things appear;
Then flow the brooks, and springs the grain,
And birds give joyful thanks for rain.

Rain, rain no more I hear,
But only bird-songs everywhere;
And rain, rain no more I see,
But shining sun on roof and tree.

# S
## Sky, Sea, Shore

Stars in a frosty sky
Crackle and blaze;
Streams in the lowland meadows
Linger and laze;
Shells on the seashore gleam,
Washed by the tide;
Seagulls over the harbour
Circle and glide.
   Blue smoke and prancing steed,
   Swallow and snake and swan—
   How many more
   Curving, glistening S-things
   In sky, sea, shore?

# T
## Tarlingwell

A town of ten towers
Is Tarlingwell,
And in every tower
There hangs a bell.

At twelve by the clock
What a ding-dang-dell
Sounds from the towers
Of Tarlingwell!

Over the broad
And blustery weald
So many voices
Never pealed.

Harsh or mellow,
Cracked or sound,
They tell the people
For miles around

That Tarlingwell
With its ten towers tall
Still stands, whatever
Else may fall.

# U
## Un

Uncut is your corn, Farmer Hearn,
Unstacked your hay.
Unfed, your fifteen pigs
Have run away.

Unpaid are your men, Farmer Hearn,
Unpainted your byre.
Unswept is your kitchen floor,
Unlit your fire.

Unmade is your bed, Farmer Hearn,
Uncombed your hair;
You have gone with the gypsy-men
Off to the fair.

Fiddling and sing-song, Farmer Hearn,
They're the ruin of you.
When unkind winter blows
What will you do?

# V
## Vain

===

Vain is the Princess Vara,
  Her mother's eldest daughter.
She looks all day in the mirror
  As a swan in the smooth water.

Her eyes are blue like the waves,
  Her skin is soft and fair;
Red-gold like the autumn leaves
  And thick and long is her hair.

And all for her pride and beauty,
  Gold hair and eyes of blue,
From far-off court and city
  The young men come to woo.

But to none will she answer Yes,
  For none but herself loves she,
Gazing all day in the glass
  With her eyes like the lonely sea.

# W
## Words

In woods are words.
You hear them all,
Winsome, witless or wise,
When the birds call.

In woods are words.
If your ears wake
You hear them, quiet and clear,
When the leaves shake.

In woods are words.
You hear them all
Blown by the wet wind
When raindrops fall.

In woods are words
Kind or unkind;
Birds, leaves and hushing rain
Bring them to mind.

# X
## X-roads

Besides the cross-roads on the hill
With crossed sails stands the mill
   That once ground corn to make men bread.
Up to that hill two armies came
With crossed swords to fight for fame.
   Night fell on many brave men dead.

These are the words the four winds cried:
'Fame is a shadow: vain is pride;
   Trampled cornfields will not grow.'
Now if those men had ceased from strife
And harkened to the winds of life,
   They would have lived to plough and sow.

# Y
## Yonder

Through yonder park there runs a stream;
By yonder stream there sits a man;
As yonder man in silence sits
He catches fish as best he can.

While yonder fish, one, two and three,
Through yonder limpid waters steer,
Why does yon silent fisherman
Drop first a sigh and then a tear?

Why does he cast yon fishing-line
Again, again, and all for nought?
It is because yon little fish,
For all his care, will *not* be caught.

# Z
## Zachary Zed

Zachary Zed was the last man,
  The last man left on earth.
For everyone else had died but him
  And no more come to birth.

In former times young Zachary
  Had asked a maid to wed.
'I loves thee, dear,' he told her true,
  'Will thou be Missis Zed?'

'No, not if you was the last man
  On earth!' the maid replied:
And he was; but she wouldn't give consent,
  And in due time she died.

So all alone stood Zachary.
  ''Tis not so bad,' he said,
'There's no one to make me brush my hair
  Nor send me up to bed.

'There's none can call me wicked,
  Nor none to argufy,
So dang my soul if I don't per-nounce
  LONG LIVE KING ZACHAR-Y!'

So Zachary Zed was the last man
  And the last King beside,
And never a person lived to tell
  If ever Zachary died.

# The Story
## of
# Jackie Thimble

# The Story of Jackie Thimble

There was a boy called Jackie Thimble,
And he was thought both neat and nimble:
His height was one foot four.
Yes, sixteen inches was his height—
Just think of it—a tot, a mite,
No taller than a riding boot,
No longer than a marrow!

But he was cheerful as a flute,
And cheeky as a sparrow.

And he would sing, and hop, and caper,
And hide behind the morning paper,
Or underneath a pudding-bowl—
Or creep inside a rabbit-hole
Or balance on a saucepan-lid—
Why, there's no time
To tell you half the things he did:
For Jackie was so very small—
Remember! scarcely sixteen inches tall.

But Jackie's parents were both old and poor;
They hardly had enough
To keep the wolf away from their back door
When times were rough.
They never could make both ends meet,
They never had enough to eat.

Their home was in a narrow street
And, though it was both clean and neat,
In winter it was deathly cold,

For it was but an attic;
And Mrs Thimble she was stiff with cold;
And Mr Thimble was rheumatic.

Now Jackie was their only child.
Though he was cheeky, he was good;
He liked a joke but was not wild
And helped as best he could.
He lit the fire, and cleaned the shoes;
He skipped about with talk and news,
And sang or whistled half the day;
He swept the floor and laid the table;
In short, he did what he was able.

To make his parents glad and gay.
And so, in spite of their distress,
They loved him well, as you may guess.

Though they were old and mousy poor
And felt the winter's pinch,
And he was only one foot four,
They loved him, every inch.
So all were happy in their way,
Until one DREADFUL DAY.

Jackie Thimble disappeared.
Oh, how his mother cried and groaned!
And how his poor old father feared!
The snow fell thick, the north wind moaned.
They searched the attic low and high,
They looked in chests and cupboards,
They searched the loft, they searched the larder—
It was as bare as Mother Hubbard's.
There was no trace—the hours went by;
The evening came, the wind blew harder.
Distracted with their grief and care,
The two poor folks ran here and there—
The boy was nowhere to be found.
They thought he must be dead;
And when at last the night came round,
They sadly went to bed.

But (are you listening everyone?)
If only they had seen their son,
They would have laughed for joy instead,
For Jackie was by no means dead.
And if you listen hard, I'll tell
What curious things to him befell.
It happened, that particular day,
That Jackie had gone out to play.
As carelessly he wandered on
Through streets and alleys big and small,
He chanced to see a pillar-box,
And it was round, and red, and tall.

The postman's van was standing near.
The pillar-box was open wide;
The postman had not closed the door,
So Jackie Thimble peeped inside.
'What fun,' he thought, 'to clamber in!'
It was so dark, and tall, and round.
The postman in the postman's van
Was stowing mail-bags safe and sound.
So Jackie climbed into the box
Unseen, and started to explore.
What fun to go where no one's been before!
Remember, he was only one foot four.

He felt like Scott discovering the Pole;
He felt like Livingstone and Mungo Park;
Here he would meet no other living soul,
And darkest Africa was not so dark.
Oh, he had always wanted to explore!
Just then—
            the postman shut the door!

The door slammed to; the lock was fast.
Jackie Thimble gave a shout.
'Hi, Mr Postman,' Jackie cried,
'Let me out!—Please, let me out!'
In vain. The postman paid no heed,
He, poor man, was hard of hearing;
So Jackie, with a beating heart,
Heard the mail-van disappearing.
He shouted loud, but none was near
His anxious cries to overhear;

And so to keep his courage strong,
Poor Jackie raised his voice in song:
'The Minstrel Boy' and 'Scots Wha Ha'e,'
'Boys and Girls, Come Out to Play,'
'Cockles and Mussels,' 'Linden Lea,'
'Here's a Health unto Her Majesty,'
'Home, Sweet Home,' 'The First Noel.'
He sang them all both clear and well.
He sang them all with might and main,
And then he sang them through again.

Now Mrs Cox and Miss de Vere
Were two old ladies living near;
And they were hurrying home together
At tea-time through the winter weather.
It happened that they passed along
As Jack was finishing a song.

'Why, gracious me!' said Miss de Vere.
'If you could hear what I can hear—
I do declare, dear Mrs Cox,
We've found a singing pillar-box!'
Said Mrs Cox to Miss de Vere:
'I do believe you're right, my dear.
I quite distinctly heard it sing.
I've never known the like before;
It must be fairies caroling.
For sixpence they may sing some more!'
So saying, generous Mrs Cox
Dropped sixpence in the pillar-box.
Jackie, to show his gratitude,
Began, more prettily than ever,
'There is a Tavern in the Town;'
Then Miss de Vere said, 'Well, I never!'
And sent three pennies rolling down.
'Why, bless me! it's begun to snow.'
Said Mrs Cox. 'We'd better go.'
The ladies soon told other folks
About the singing pillar-box,
And people came from far and near
So rare a miracle to hear.

'Upon our souls!' they cried. 'How funny!
A pillar-box that sings for money.'
So, as the sixpences and coppers
Came rattling down, one two, one two,
Jackie Thimble raised his voice
And sang out all the songs he knew.
Some people were afraid, and some
Could scarcely tear themselves away;
And others hurried home to tell
The marvellous thing they'd heard that day,
The strangest thing they'd ever seen—
A kind of singing slot-machine.
At last when it was cold and dark,
And folk no longer stopped to hark,
Poor Jack was feeling tired and lonely.
'How glad I'd be,' he thought, 'If only
Someone would come and let me out!'
With that he gave a feeble shout.
But no one heard. 'Oh dear,' he thought,
'I might as well be drowned.'
At last—to cut the story short—
He heard a welcome sound.
The postman's van—yes, there it was
Coming in that direction,
At ten o'clock, through hail and snow,
To make the last collection!
The postman stops the van—unlocks
The steel door of the pillar-box;
Jack wastes no time—on nimble feet
Leaps out and scurries down the street.
In half an hour, if not before,
He's knocking at his own front door.
Imagine his fond parents' joy
To see their long-lost only boy!
Their hearts are full: so are Jack's pockets.
'Look here,' cries he, 'at what I've earned!'

They laugh to see the bright, round coins,
And weep to see their boy returned.
Says Jack: 'I'm home, so don't you cry.
Just think what all these coins will buy!
Let winter days be long and bleak,
Here's fire and food for many a week.'
Then Jack begins to tell his story,
Till his old mother cries, 'Why, glory!
It's after midnight! Off to bed!
You'll never get to sleep at all!'
So ends the tale of Jackie Thimble
Who was so smart and small,
He climbed into a pillar-box to sing.
Now, did you ever hear of such a thing?

# *More*
# *Prefabulous*
# *Animiles*

*To*
*Philip*
*and Gelda Ardizzone*

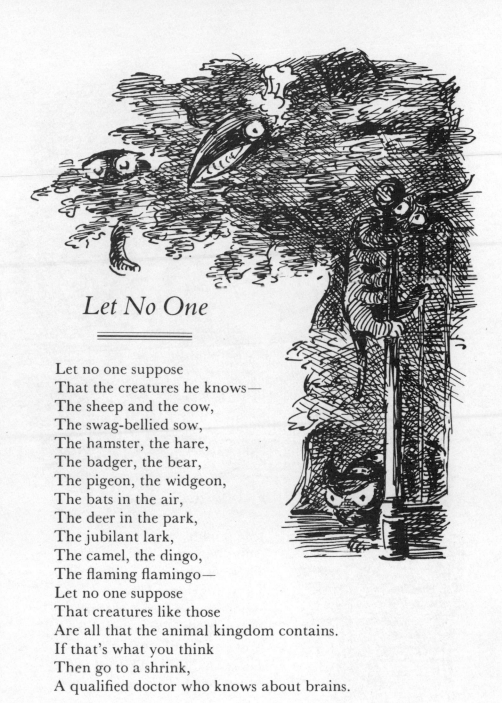

## Let No One

Let no one suppose
That the creatures he knows—
The sheep and the cow,
The swag-bellied sow,
The hamster, the hare,
The badger, the bear,
The pigeon, the widgeon,
The bats in the air,
The deer in the park,
The jubilant lark,
The camel, the dingo,
The flaming flamingo—
Let no one suppose
That creatures like those
Are all that the animal kingdom contains.
If that's what you think
Then go to a shrink,
A qualified doctor who knows about brains.

When night is approaching
And poachers are poaching,
There are creatures that lurk,
They linger and lurk
When you're trying to work.
You're as pale as your book
And you hardly dare look.
There's a SOMETHING there
At the head of the stair.

202

Its breathing is slow and its odour is musky,
And its paws you are sure must be horny and husky
And everywhere's dusky
And you think if you turn on the light,
It might bite, it might smite,
It might cackle or whimper
Or whinney or simper
Or laugh.
If anyone thinks that the gracious giraffe
Is the tallest,
The microbe the smallest,
The serpent the longest,
The lion the strongest,
The cheetah the quickest,
If anyone thinks that the donkey's the thickest
Of creatures on earth, he had best think again,
For animal annals are known to contain
The records of creatures quite different from these,
Faster and vaster,
Milder and wilder,
Louder and longer
And thicker and stronger
Than any you've seen on the box or in books.
So if any suppose that the creatures he knows
Are all that the animal world can discover,
Let him turn this page over
And there he will see what the experts agree,
When they leaf through their notebooks and
    thumb through their files,
Are breath-stopping, eye-popping ANIMILES,
Your actual PREFABULOUS ANIMILES!

# The Ozalid

The Ozalid is not a thing
   I greatly care to meet.
Its neck is like a piece of string;
   Its ears are on its feet.

Its single eye is on a swivel;
   This way and that it spins.
Its smudgy nose is apt to snivvle;
   It has three flipperfins.

It has three flipperfins, my friend;
   Its tail is three feet long,
And at its hard and horny end
   It has a fatal prong—

A fatal but a useful prong,
  With which it spikes its prey,
The agile tape-fish lean and long,
  The chipworm sad and grey.

But once (I tremblingly relate)
  An Ozalid had the luck—
The evil luck, the groojus fate—
  To spear a sleeping duck.

Enraged, the duck took instant wing.
  Its flight was straight and strong.
The Ozalid, that hapless thing,
  Could not withdraw its prong.

Hung by its tail beneath the bird,
  The Ozalid soared aloft.
Cries of amazement soon were heard
  From Hull to Lowestoft.

When folks at Folkestone saw the sight
  They clamoured 'How absurd
To see an Ozalid in flight
  Transported by a bird!'

## The Troke

I celebrate the various Troke.
   'Why "various"?' I hear you cry.
Be patient, dears, and hold your smoke*,
   For I to you will make reply,
Giving you reasons multifarious
Why this strange beast is known as various.

  * 'hold your smoke' means much the same as 'hold your
fire, wait'. There is no fire without smoke, so why not 'Hold
your smoke'?

208

His hide is various, for a start,
  Being yellowish with purple bars
And spots and dots of divers hue
  And other sorts of stripes and stars.
Towards the coming on of night
He is a rather daunting sight.

But that's not all. He has four legs,
  One long, three short—or *vice versa*.
He moves in circles, more or less
  Now right, now left; and, what is worser,
His feet are ill-assorted too—
One rough, three smooth, two pink, two blue.

Sometimes he huffs, as if in anger,
　　Sometimes he shlurps in amorous vein.
When hungry, he's inclined to whindle;
　　The moon evokes a different strain:
Then hear the high nocturnal tone
That freezes all your flesh to stone.

In mood and temper too, I hear,
　　None is more various than the Troke.
At times he sulks in gloomiest dudgeon,
　　At times enjoys a simple joke.
But if you laugh at him, my dears,
He'll *snip* you like a pair of shears.

His diet too is heterogeneous
    (Or 'mixed', to use a simpler word)—
One day he wants no food but nuts,
    Next day it's mice; but on the third
A rival Troke he's apt to slaughter,
Or else he'll fast and live on water.

He is not loved, I must confess,
    Among the Animile community.
He is too unpredictable,
    His life has neither use nor unity.
I tolerate, but would not stroke,
The broody, moody, various Troke.

## The Dizz

Oh, have you seen the beauteous Dizz
And heard his soft 'Biz-biz! biz-biz!'
As through the sumptious evening hour
He oscillates from flower to flower.
His long discerning nose can tell
The difference of smell from smell,
As on his busy way he goes
From honeybunch to sugarose.

He has six wings, not all the same,
Two mauve, two emerald, two flame,
On which he trundles here and there
All in the sumptious summer air,
Or with his plushy wings spread wide
He does the gorgeous glitterglide,
Something between a dive and dance,
Which puts the watchers in a trance.
'It is,' they sigh, 'it is, it is
The ultraspecial, long-nosed Dizz.

The Queen Dizz has no wings at all,
But sits at home in Honey Hall
Enjoying the galooshus things
Her ever-helpful helpmeet brings.
How fortunate if *you* should spy
So rare a creature in the sky
And hear the soft 'Biz-biz! biz-biz!'
Emitted by the beauteous Dizz.
Oh, how his six wings whirr and whizz!

# The Kwackagee

Back in the bleak and blurry days
When all was murk and mystery—
That is (if I may mint a phrase)
Before the dawn of history.
Professors think there used to be,
Not far from Waikee-waike,
A monster called the Kwackagee,
A sort of flying snake.

This animile, they all agree,
Was forty feet in length,
Would spiral up the tallest tree
And then with all his strength
Propel himself with sinuous grace
And undulation muscular
To find another feeding-place
In some far vale crepuscular.

Expert opinions are two
About his mode of travel;
Professor Grommit holds one view;
The other, Doctor Gravvle.
Grommit believes he could give off
Some kind of speed-emulsion;
The Doctor, ever prone to scoff,
Postulates jet-propulsion.

In prehistoric Waikee-waike,
The men (if men there were),
Would they in breathless terror quake
To hear that rattling whirr
As flew the monster through the sky?
Or would they brave the foe
With missile and with battle-cry?—
The experts do not know.

# *The Nog*

The fragrant vale of Chatnagog
Harbours the small and sprightly Nog.
His shape is oval, like an egg;
He has one short and springy leg,
On which, though he himself is small—
No bigger than a croquet ball—
He bounces a prodigious way
Here, there and everywhere all day,
Six, seven or eight feet at a bound,
Sometimes in mid-air twirling round
Or somersaulting high as high
All in the blue and boiling sky.

The Nog is an endearing fellow.
His shining skin is lemon yellow.
His mate is of a duller hue,
But she, like him, can trill and coo;
Like him she chirrups as she bounces,
But if some direful danger pounces
The dog-toothed hawk of Chatnagog
Or, even worse, the hawk-toothed dog,

A sharp, shrill twitter of alarm
Gives notice of impending harm.
That instant she will lie as still
As stones upon a desert hill,
Whose colour she will imitate,
Huddled beside her trusty mate.
But when no peril hovers near,
From lurking foe the coast is clear,

In short, when all is safe once more,
Why then the cry is 'Vive le sport!'
(I quote in French the exclamation
In tribute to this sporting nation.)
Then down the fragrant valley see
Both Nog and Noglets bouncing free,
Grown-ups and children, old and young.
Now let him spring who never sprung!

(Well yes, I know—it should be 'sprang' . . .)
You never saw so spry a gang
As gather for the bouncing races
From near and far and other places;
And many a sporting writer names
The Chatnagog Olympic games
As much the jolliest of the season.
I must admit they have good reason.

But not without a sense of shame
I must describe a different game.
Some boy Nogs, bigger than the rest—
'Them Noggoes' they are called in jest—
These boy Nogs of the ruder sort
Without a proper sense of sport
Engage in what they call 'Nog bowls',
In which by turns each player rolls
A Noglet to a central spot
Where sits an old Nog called 'the pot'.
With raucous glee the Noggoes roll
The Noglets to the 'pot' or goal.
This game the Noglets do not like
And are prepared to go on strike.
In time the older Nogs, no doubt,
Will stamp the cruel practice out,
That such things shall no more disgrace
This cheerful, harmless, sprightly race,
And innocent mirth alone resound
In Chatnagog's delightful ground.

# The Hoverwing

Italians think there's nothing sweeter
Than what they call the *dolce vita*,
While other folk—and they are plenty—
Extol the *Dolce far niente*.
The Boo-boos of the Blissful Ocean
Express a similar emotion
When, basking by their sandy caves,
They contemplate the wimbling waves.
From care and pain their lives are free;
They fish for fish upon the sea;
When skies are clear and winds are calm,
They climb the graceful pogo palm

In quest of its galooshus fruit
With which they eat the gah-gah root.
But, as I said, their dearest wish
Is on the sea to fish for fish—
The salamo, the polypod,
The megaprawn, the blue-nosed cod
And other denizens of savour,
Some for their texture, some their flavour.

Ah me! there is no way of life
Without its special source of strife,
Without the occasional disappointment.
Such is the blow-fly in the ointment;
Such is the maggot in the peach,
The broken bottle on the beach.
What garden is without a weed?

—Enough of this. Let me proceed:
Even the Boo-boos have a woe;
It is that dire-destructive foe;
It is that most horrendous thing,
The greater saw-backed Hoverwing.
A larger version of the whale,
It has a forked and furious tail;
Its sickening, oleaginous stench

Can make the sturdiest seaman blench;
Its hide repels the sharpest spear;
Its bellow fills the best with fear;
Its roar is like a hurricane.
Its forty spouts can drown in rain
The biggest craft constructed yet
And smaller vessels overset,
So cataclysmic the commotion

Occasioned on the Blissful Ocean
By that most ultra-groojus thing,
The greater saw-backed Hoverwing.
See how it somersaults and spins,
Gyrating on its turbo-fins.
See how it wallows, skims and flies,
Descending from pacific skies
To swamp their boats and terrorize
With hoarse and blood-congealing cries
The harmless Boo-boos, whose sole wish
Is but to bask and fish for fish.

You in your safe retreat may smile
To read about this animile,
But spare a thought, I do implore,
For those who, by the Blissful shore,
Pursue their harmless avocation,
The childlike, simple Boo-boo nation.

# The Bogus-Boo

The Bogus-boo
Is a creature who
Comes out at night—and why?
He likes the air;
He likes to scare
The nervous passer-by.

Out from the park
At dead of dark
He comes with huffling pad.
If, when alone,
You hear his moan,
'Tis like to drive you mad.

He has two wings,
Pathetic things,
With which he cannot fly.
His tusks look fierce,
Yet could not pierce
The merest butterfly.

He has six ears,
But what he hears
Is very faint and small;
And with the claws
On his eight paws
He cannot scratch at all.

He looks so wise
With his owl-eyes,
His aspect grim and ghoulish;
But truth to tell,
He sees not well
And is distinctly foolish.

This Bogus-boo,
What can he do
But huffle in the dark?
So don't take fright;
He has no bite
And very little bark.

# The Sniggle

The Sniggle (often called the Snyle)
Is not a lovely animile.
He has four legs equipped with claws,
Another six with sucker-paws.
When thus he climbs up walls of rock,
You hear his suckers go *plick-plock*.
*Plick-plock plick-plock*—by night he crawls
On gutter-pipes and roofs and walls.
The Sniggle's is a groujus noise,
Dreaded by all offending boys.

The Sniggle lurks in Woeful Woods
And noses out his favourite foods—
The slow-worm and the blunderbug,
The slurp, the giant hairy slug,
Also that most galooshus dish,
The frozocrumm or finger-fish.

The full-grown adult Snyle (or Sniggle)
Has one long horn which he can wiggle,
Emitting a ferocious bray
With which to terrorize his prey.
When terrorized himself, the Snyle
Secretes a black and fexious bile.
The men who flourished long ago

Beside the River Gallimo
Use it to smear upon their skins
To scare away the gobbolins.
Others, for more artistic ends,
Employed it to surprise their friends
By making abstract wall designs
In flowing and expressive lines.

Noxious as is the Sniggle male,
To see his mate your heart would fail,
For she is squalid, squat and small.
She has no bile, no claws at all;
Her horn is short and will not wiggle,
Her only note a nervous giggle.
She lives on scraps her mate supplies.
I say in short, and none denies,
The female Sniggle is a creature
Without a sole redeeming feature.
So I conclude with jubilation
This sad, this groojus recitation.

# The Pickadile

Far in the land of Waikee-waike
Among the trees by Happi Lake
There lives a curious Animile—
To wit, the fragrant Pickadile.
The denizens of Waikee-waike
Pursue him for his perfume's sake.
This perfume is a cross between
Lemon verbena and quinine.
Bees, butterflies, small birds as well
Are drawn towards the sumptious smell.
This satisfies the creature's pride
For he is somewhat dandified.
This superelegant Animile
Is fashioned in rococo style.

His smile is devious and dental;
His limbs are lithe and ornamental;
On two he walks, or rather glides,
And two hang drooping at his sides,
Except when he is culling flowers,
Which, when he's hungry, he devours.
His scaly tail is long and strong;
With it, when roused, *'bing-bong! bing-bong!'*

A battery of telling blows
He rains upon all jealous foes.
But, truth to tell, he has not many.
A pair of sinuous antennae
Protrude from out his fulgious curls,
And these he preens, he pranks, he twirls.
With a tall tuft his top is decked,
Plumy, curvaceous and erect.

If you should go to Waikee-waike
And stroll beside the Happi Lake,
Observe this fragrant Animile,
The condescending Pickadile

As joysomely he trots and trips,
A sprightly *chanson* on his lips—
That is to say, upon his beak;
His voice is but a groojus squeak.

Now lesser creatures jeer at him;
They find his manner proud and prim;
They imitate his sinuous grace
And make rude noises to his face.
But all their efforts fail to rile
The odoriferous Pickadile.
Long may he glide by Happi Lake
In the far land of Waikee-waike.

# The Oxyphantasorius

From times prefabulous and now long gone
The Oxyphantasorius lingers on
In deserts far from human habitation.
He is the hugest creature in creation.
His blood-congealing, grim, and bulbous figure
Is something like an elephant's, but bigger;

In shape and size the Oxyphantasorius
Has been described as *almost henrymoorius*.
Compared with him, the whale is but a sprat,
The crocodile a frog, the crow a gnat;
Compared with him, etcetera, etcetera . . .
(Make up the rest yourself, and do it betterer.)
He has a trunk, two deadly tusks, three humps,
A muscular, broad tail with which he jumps
After the manner of a kangaroo.
They tried to trap him for a private zoo,
But had to give it up; he jumped too high.
His roar would make a sergeant-major cry.
There are no ears for those Wagnerian tones,
The blaring of a thousand saxophones.
Even the master-minds at Tunbridge Wells
Could not compute those murderous decibels.

All is a wilderness where he inhabits;
All creatures cower and flee like hunted rabbits.
So how he lives remains a mystery.
Some say he feeds upon the yumyum tree;
Some say he jumps upon the native villages
Beyond the desert, which the monster pillages
And, putting the inhabitants to flight,
He gluts his juggernautical appetite.
At all events, the oxyphantasorius
Is judged by naturalists to be uxorious;
In other words the creature wants to find
A spouse with whom to propagate his kind:
It is not hunger makes him so uproarious—
He needs a female Oxyphantasorius.
This, say the experts, is what drives him on,
This late survivor from times dead and gone.

Oh what a fate were ours should he succeed
And overrun the planet with his breed!
Perish the thought; perish this nightmare too,
This oxyphantile crypto-kangaroo.
So let your prayers be lengthy and laborious
To exorcise the Oxyphantasorius.
God Save Her Majesty! Send her victorious
Against her foe, the Oxyphantasorius.

# Additional
# Poems

# Domenico

Domenico, Domenico,
Why have you let me down?
You promised me a silken dress
When last you went to town.
But all you bring is a cotton thing,
A dress of common blue –
I like you well, Domenico,
Why have you let me down?

Domenico, Domenico,
Why did you let me down?
You promised me a china spaniel,
Gold and pink and brown.
But all you bring is a shivering thing,
A half-starved mongrel pup –
I like you well, Domenico,
Why do you let me down?

Domenico, Domenico,
Again you've let me down,
You promised me a golden harp
To finger up and down.
But all you bring is a paltry thing,
A whistle of rusty tin –
I like you well Domenico,
But you always let me down.

Domenico, Domenico,
I'll wear my dress of blue,
My mongrel pup shall follow me,
And I will follow you,
As you blow the whistle of rusty tin
And beg for pennies brown –
I love you so, Domenico,
Why must you let me down?

# The Ballad of Gideon

This is the song of Gideon,
Of Gideon brave and cunning,
Who took no sword but the sword of the Lord
When he sent the foeman running.
Now the sword of the Lord and of Gideon
Had neither hilt nor blade.
Bend down your ear if you would hear
Of what that sword was made.

For seven years the children of God
Had served the Midianite,
When to Gideon under Gideon's tree
Appeared an angel bright.
From out of the oak the angel spoke,
As clear as the sun's meridian:
'Go forth, thou man of valour strong,
And smite the hosts of Midian!'

'I have no sword,' said Gideon.
'I am no man of might;
But I and thirty thousand men
Will rout the Midianite.'
'You need no sword,' the angel said,
'If you have brain and nerve;
You need not thirty thousand men,
Three hundred men will serve.

Let them go forth by dark of night
With you to be their guide.
Let each man take an earthen pot
With a lighted lamp inside.
Let each man bear a trumpet
To blow at your command.
And *this* is the sword, the sword of the Lord,
Shall be in each man's hand.'

Thus the angel spoke from Gideon's oak,
And Gideon rose that night.
And went with his three hundred men
To put their foes to flight;
Ahead went cunning Gideon
With God to be his guide,
And each man had an earthen pot
With a lighted lamp inside;

In each man's hand a trumpet,
And silent as a ghost,
The children of the Lord crept down,
About the sleeping host.
Then Gideon smashed his earthen pot
And waved his lamp on high,
Blew on his ram's-horn loud and harsh
And gave the battle-cry.

Three hundred pots were shattered;
Three hundred trumpets brayed:
Small wonder that the Midianites
Awoke and were dismayed!
For the music that they heard that night
Was neither soft not lydian –
Those fearful tones that chilled their bones,
Those brazen strains that froze their veins,
That piercing cry that split the sky:
THE SWORD OF THE LORD AND OF GIDEON!
THE SWORD OF THE LORD AND OF GIDEON!
THE SWORD OF THE LORD AND OF GIDEON!

In terror and confusion
The heathen host arose;
But dazed by light and stunned by noise
They could not strike their foes.
Some drew their swords on one another,
Some fled into the night:
And thus three hundred unarmed men
Put all that host to flight.

So ends the song of Gideon,
Of Gideon brave and cunning,
Who took no sword but the sword of the Lord
And sent the foeman running.
Faithful and few, the sons of God
Are always a match for Midian
So long as they hold that weapon bold,
The sword of the Lord and of Gideon.


# Gliders and Gulls

What are they, these gliders in the blue, cold air,
Riders
On the unseen fields of the air?
These are the gulls. See how they rise on
The clouds' snow mountains, soar
To the grey horizon, stand on the air,
Then with a twitch of their white sails dive,
Down dive to the spray-drenched stone-strewn shore,
Dive, down dive, beak first, to the spume-topped wave,
Home of the fish,
White-bellied, stripe-backed fish.

What are these other birds,
These giant birds,
Launched from the green heights,
The green heights of the downs, racehorses
On the sky's twelve winds, the sky's racecourses?
These are the gliders,
They bear their riders to a freedom not of earth.

261

Stately over the wide world drift these gliders.
Their shadows move across the wheatfields,
The straight canals, the car-parks, the playgrounds.
The children look up, shading their eyes to see
What winged wonder hovers over their play.

See how gulls and gliders
Carve for themselves invisible statues of freedom
With the chisel-blades of their wings
In the limitless spaces of air.

# Do What You Will

As soon command the snow in August,
As soon deny the winds of March
As tell young Guy and Gideon Hargest
To hush beneath the railway arch.

They run, they jump, they volley stones,
They shout their names, they shout 'Hulloo!'
The archway echoes their shrill tones,
And answers with 'Hulloo – oo – ooo!'

As soon forbid the rain in April,
The birds at dawn cry 'Chirra-wirra'
As order Gwen and Gwynneth Capel
To disregard the bedroom mirror.

They preen, they prank, they whisper, chirrup,
They rouge, they powder, point a shoe,
And brush their hair as smooth as syrup.
They do just what they want to do.

The snows that freeze, the sun that blisters,
The birds that brave the charging sea
Say to all brothers and all sisters,
'Do what you will, while you are free.'

# Poor Jenny's Song

Spell me a spell, Mister Doctor,
To cure my wretched cold.
And I will give you silver,
But I won't give you gold
To cure my wretched cold.

Spell me a spell, Mister Doctor,
To cure my heart of love.
I will give you a silver bird,
Likewise a golden dove,
To cure my heart of love.

Spell me a spell, Mister Doctor,
To cure my deadly grief.
I gave my heart to a young man
Turned out to be a thief,
Which caused me deadly grief.

# Kara My Tortoise

Kara my tortoise has a horny back.
Her colour varies between brown and black.
Lettuce she loves and, next to lettuce, grapes.
How charming in the sun to see her traipse
Across the lawn to find a warmer spot.
Now, truth to tell, my tortoise Kara's not
Demonstrative, affectionate or fond :
To my endearments she does not respond.
I call her name, I stroke, I coo, bleat;
She sighs, and agitates her four feet.
'I want,' she seems to say, 'to be alone.
I wish I were what I am like – a stone.'
In autumn, long before December's frost,
It seems her one desire is to get lost.
Under the soil she goes where I can't find her,
But she will reappear when spring is kinder.

# Gabble-Gabble

'Gabble-Gabble! gabble-gabble!'
The seven fat geese say.
'Gabble-gabble! gabble-gabble!'
In the green field all day.

'Gabble-gabble' – never stopping,
While the sun sweeps the sky.
Gabble-gabble go the seven geese,
And I will tell you why.

Those seven geese sat in the hot sun
In the meadow long ago,
And through the hedge came the red fox
And spied them all in a row.

'Ho ho!' said he with a wicked grin
And a glint in his hungry eye,
'I never saw such a dinner before,
And today those geese must die!'

'Oh no, Sir Fox, have pity on us!'
They cried with anguish shrill.
'Sir Fox,' they begged, 'it is not right
Such poor weak birds to kill.'

'Fat, foolish geese, your wailing cease,'
Said the red fox in his greed.
'Fat, foolish geese, prepare to die;
Your plaints I will not heed.'

'Oh then, Sir Fox,' the first goose said,
'If our lives you will spare,
Take us and eat us one and all,
But first let us say a prayer.

'Gladly we give ourselves to you
When we have prayed to Heaven
For we shall be the sweeter fare
If our sins be forgiven.'

'A pious thought,' the fox agreed.
'Pray on, pray on, I say!
I will not touch you, foolish geese,
Till you have ceased to pray.'

So 'gabble-gabble' the seven geese prayed
From sunrise to sunset.
'Gabble-gabble' to Heaven they cried
And have not left off yet.

# Alexander

Alexander played with his bricks on the floor –
Square bricks, pointed bricks, red, green and white.
He tried to build a castle with a tower and battlements,
He tried to build a castle but it wouldn't come right.

He tried to build a castle with a dungeon and drawbridge
(Alexander with his bricks on the floor),
But it turned into a supermarket with a car-park,
So he knocked it over and started once more.

He tried to build a church with a pointed doorway,
He tried to build a church with a gold weather-vane,
But it turned to a multi-storey grand hotel,
So he knocked it over and started again.

Alexander tried to build a lighthouse
To rescue ships from storm-racked tide,
But it turned to a factory for making boxes.
Alexander put away his bricks and cried.

# Index